# Mindset

## How Positive Thinking Will Set You Free & Help You Achieve Massive Success In Your Life

# Mindset:

Benjamin Smith

Published by Benjamin smith, 2016.

MINDSET:

**First edition. January 4, 2016.**

Copyright © 2016 Benjamin Smith.

ISBN: 978-1393861652

Written by Benjamin Smith.

# Benjamin Smith

# Table of Contents

# Introduction

I want to thank you and congratulate you for downloading the book, "MINDSET- How Positive Thinking Will Set You Free & Help You Achieve Massive Success In Your Life".

This book will help you learn how to embrace positive thinking in order to achieve success in your life.

Since you're reading this, it's safe to assume that you have concerns about your mindset in life. Maybe you think you're too pessimistic. You might have trouble achieving goals or moving forward in work and school. It can be really difficult to figure out why you are having these struggles. You are doing the best thing you possibly can; you've taken the first step in recognizing that your mindset may be influencing how you approach the challenges you face.

Do you ever wonder why some people get to achieve their dreams whereas some people never even get close to that? It can be challenging to reach your goals, and that challenge is normal. But you may be experiencing more than just challenges. If you are constantly second guessing yourself, doubting your worth, and criticizing yourself, you're adding a level of difficulty to your goals. You may not even realize you're doing this. So, what makes the difference between someone who seems to get things done, achieve success, and seem to have it all and someone who does not seem to get things done? Well, the one thing that has a huge impact on whether you pursue your dreams or not is your mind.

Our minds are in charge of much more than just our physical bodies. Your thoughts have the power to influence your actions in more ways than you know. While your mind is a very powerful organ, if you don't harness its full potential, then you will not live the kind of life you desire. Think about it; when your mind believes that you are already defeated, no amount of practice or training can make you believe otherwise. In fact, even when people keep telling you that you can do it, when your mind thinks you can't, you won't make any significant progress in whatever it is you wanted to do.

It's not as easy as simply thinking good thoughts. When I first started my mindfulness journey, I thought it was simply replacing negative thoughts with positive ones. I thought I could swap critical words for complementary ones and then, poof! My goals would be achievable. As I came to learn, that's just not how this works. Over the last several years, I have learned what it really takes to completely revamp the way I think. I haven't simply replaced words, I've changed my entire outlook on the world around me. How did I accomplish this? It wasn't easy, but using the tips I've laid out in this book, I was able to fix my self-doubt issues and start living my life to the most of its potential.

I learned these principles through pure trial and error. I discovered that the best way to make myself more mindful was to deliberately change my thinking patterns. When I made these changes a habit, I didn't have to constantly think about them anymore. Once I didn't have to think about them, it became second nature to act on them. I changed my thoughts, and they changed me, not the other way around. So in essence, the secret to success in life lies in harnessing the power of the mind. If you are fully aware of that but find it hard to use your mind's unlimited power to unleash your full potential, this book will help you to achieve just that.

If you are looking for actionable information on how to harness the power of the mind to transform yourself, then this book will teach you how to unleash the full power of your mindset to transform your life. I know it will help, because it's exactly what I did. I'm not the only person that has seen these tips. I showed them to my friends and family as well. The ones who actually followed them, who really put in the time to focus and change their habits, thanked me profusely. Of course, not everyone I've shown this to was as successful. If you want to change the way you think, you will need to dedicate time and effort to the process. If you do, you will transform your life for the better.

Thanks again for downloading this book, I hope you enjoy it!

# Wait! Before You Start Reading Claim Your Free Limited-Time Bonus! Visit MindsetMultiplied.Com

**About The Author**

Benjamin Smith is the Author of this best selling book and also the creator of Mindset Multiplied an online brand dedicated to helping the everyday person transform their mind for success. We hope to achieve this through our blogs, videos, and books where we create engaging and educational content to help you create a growth mindset. You can find out more about us on youtube, facebook and website.

Youtube: Mindset Multiplied
Facebook: Mindset Multiplied
Website: MindsetMultiplied.Com

Chapter 1: Why You Need to Embrace Positive Thinking

Jessica's friend, Tom, needs to go for a drive this weekend. He doesn't like driving long distances, but he has to drive five hours for work. He comes to Jessica complaining about how grueling this task is going to be.

"I hate driving so long," he starts, "I wish I could just take a flight, but work won't pay for that."

Jessica starts to respond sympathetically, but then remembers that she has been working on improving her mindset lately. She decides that maybe Tom could use this skill, too.

"Well, what parts do you not like about it, specifically?" She asks.

"First of all, I hate sitting down for so long, it makes my back ache."

She thinks for a minute, then responds, "You know, just because the drive is five hours doesn't mean you have to do the whole drive in one go. You could stop at gas stations more frequently and do some jumping jacks or jog in place so you don't have to sit as much!"

He looks thoughtful and responds, "That actually sounds like a good idea. But it wouldn't fix the boredom issues."

She has a suggestion for this one, too. "Don't think of it as boredom or wasted time, think of it as an opportunity to have some quiet space for a while. You could bring a fun audiobook or podcast, you could try to think about an issue you're having trouble solving. You'll have five hours to yourself to reflect."

"Hey," he says, smiling, "I never thought of it like that! That's a great point!"

"And if you're still dreading the trip, just remember you get to see some nice scenery you don't get in the city. Even if you're just driving past farms and empty space, you get a whole slice of landscape you never get to see in your day-to-day commute."

Now, he looks excited, "I do love seeing cows and horses when I drive, maybe I'll get to see some."

Tom leaves to go on his drive, and when he gets back, he lets Jessica know how nice the drive was.

"You know," he says, "I've always hated road trips, but that one was actually kind of fun. I got to listen to a new book, my back didn't get sore because I made stops, and I even got to see a baby horse on a ranch. How did you know to do all that?"

Jessica tells him about all the new skills she's learned to help brighten her mindset. By showing her friend the positives that replaced his negative thoughts, his entire attitude around road trips changed. She made his work life much easier, just by showing him how to shift his mindset.

It is so hard nowadays to have a positive mindset. News is filled with tragedy and frustrations, to the point where it feels healthy to stay uninformed. Why is having a positive mindset such a good thing? When everything seems bad, how do you keep your thoughts good? I'm sure you've asked yourself these questions countless times. If you're reading this book, you are actively looking for answers. Many of us wonder how to remain positive in the world today, but most people assume that they just have to deal with it. They believe that negative feelings are normal and that harmful thoughts are a part of that. While no one is happy all the time, many people know that positivity in the midst of turmoil is possible.

There are a plethora of misconceptions existing about what positive thinking actually is. Most people think positive thinking is simply tuning out the bad thoughts and ignoring anything potentially upsetting. As you will soon learn, positive thinking is a lot more than just being happy and optimistic. You can't be happy all the time, and you can't be optimistic 24 hours of every day. We all have bad moods and bitter thoughts from time to time. Positive thinking is also not naivety. People who shift their thinking habits to be more positive are not less knowledgeable or worldly; they are better at balancing their thoughts about events that happen to and around them. Before discussing how exactly to develop a positive mindset, it is essential to discuss its amazing benefits. Below are some benefits of how you stand to benefit by embracing positive thinking.

Freedom from Negative Thinking

Positive thinking liberates you and makes you free, but what precisely does it free you from? Well, by developing a positive mindset, you get freedom from all the negativity inhabiting your mind. Your negative thoughts corrupt your mind and gradually pollute your emotions, behaviour, and attitude. Thoughts like 'How can I achieve that?', 'I am incapable of doing that', 'No, I am not good enough for this', 'I am a failure', 'What if something goes wrong' and similar thoughts are negative thoughts because they instill fear in you and make you succumb to your fears. These negative thoughts prevent you from taking a step forward because they make you feel incapable of doing something. You surrender to them each time and never consider going against them. This is precisely why you stay stuck in your cocoon for life and are never able to live freely.

Negative thinking can stop your momentum in its tracks, but it can also stop you before you have the chance to start. A study of more than 30,000 people found that negative thoughts precede mental illnesses (Kinderman et al., 2013). In people who have a family history of mental illness, their negative thoughts exacerbated these diseases further. How can you expect yourself to achieve your goals when the thoughts in your own head are constantly doubting you? Negative thoughts can include self-doubt, guilt, and low self-esteem. When you are surrounding yourself with these thoughts, they become your attitude and shift the way you act, both toward yourself and others. It's surprisingly easy to develop this thought pattern without even noticing. For example, when you took tests in grade school, your teacher probably graded your work with a red pen. After a few years of this, it's easy to associate writing from red pen to mean "wrong" or "bad." Now, if you see a red pen written somewhere, it immediately tells you that you need to correct something. You may even avoid using red pens entirely because you associate it with lower grades. Your entire attitude towards red handwriting is negative, because you were trained to associate it with negative thoughts. This is exactly what happens to your own self-esteem as well. If you think you look bad every time you see yourself in the mirror, then eventually your attitude to your physical body will be that it is ugly, even when that isn't the case. When you adopt a positive mindset, you will be able to stop these thoughts in their tracks and then get rid of them before you take them seriously. Suddenly, red ink on paper is just another color. You take the negative meaning away, and the positivity is all that's left.

Brains are trainable, so you need to be careful what you teach yourself to think. Your negative mindset can lead to negative habits directed towards yourself. When you learn to undo this habit, you'll discover that you are much more capable than you let yourself believe. Your negative thoughts are like carrying around a personal bully wherever you go. This bully points out all your insecurities, makes you feel inadequate when you compare yourself to others, and blames any uncomfortable event—no matter how small—on you. Most people have had this bully with them for so long, they don't realize it's there, and therefore don't realize how nice it is to go without it. Your bully beats you down and humiliates you. The longer time goes on, the more you think the bully is telling the truth. Once you're convinced all these negative thoughts are true, that's when you start to freeze. How could you achieve a goal that you think you're incapable of achieving? How should you expect yourself to be assertive around others when you're constantly putting yourself down? Many people struggle with these negative thought patterns and don't realize that they are lies. This personal bully is now responsible for all the places that you feel you've failed in life. But you haven't failed, you're just listening to the wrong thoughts. As you learn to eliminate negative thoughts, that bully will have less and less power. You'll take away its ability to insult you. You have this ability already, you just haven't applied it to your own thoughts. For example, have you ever given your child a punishment and they lash out at you, saying how they hate you and how mad they are at you? Do you believe them? Of course not! You know that children don't fully understand the actions of the adults around them, especially if they want something that will harm them, such as an unhealthy snack. As a parent, even when your child says these things, you know they only say it in anger, and you don't take it to heart. You are more mature than them. When you do this, you are using your ability to ignore negative thoughts. You have the capacity to do this with your own thoughts as well; you just haven't been taught how.

Not only are your negative thoughts harming your mind, they hurt your body, too. Stress, anxiety, and depression are all illnesses caused by these negative thoughts that can lead to physical harm. If you ever wonder just how much stress can affect your life, look at pictures of US presidents before and after they served as President. Just eight years in one of the most demanding jobs in the world can age someone decades. Stress can cause bodily issues that are superficial, such as your hair turning gray, but it can be substantial, too. Heart issues and mental illnesses can be caused by stress. Mental illnesses can lead to things such as palpitations, self-harm, or eating disorders that further harm your body. And all these things are caused by that little bully people carry around. Negative thoughts stress you out and make you feel lonely and inadequate, and you start believing them. Pretty soon, you change your behavior to match the thoughts and lies in your life. If your negative thoughts tell you that you are overweight, you may start eating less and end up malnourished. If your thoughts are telling you that you are a mean person, you may stop spending time with people, leading to loneliness. These thoughts have huge physical ramifications that are very hard to ignore. And if you don't know why, how can you even begin to address these issues?

However, by learning to develop a positive mindset, you learn to battle the negative thoughts emerging inside you. Positive thinking helps you realize that your ill thoughts, feelings, and emotions are nothing, but a corruption of normal thoughts. There isn't anything you cannot do; it is just a matter of trying. With time, your positive mindset helps to liberate you from the negativity rooted inside you, making you strong enough to stand on your own and put an end to pessimism for once. As soon as you are able to shatter the negative mindset, you find out that life is indeed very beautiful and simple. Hence, the biggest benefit of a positive mindset is to provide you with complete freedom from negativity that stops you from chasing your dreams and goals.

Help you See Possibilities in Life

In addition to freeing you from your negative thoughts, positive thinking helps you become free and liberated by helping you see the different possibilities in life. Research has proven that a negative mindset compels you to behave in a specified manner only. When you have a negative thought, this makes you frightened of a certain outcome and restricts you from taking any action against that outcome. Hence, you cannot go beyond that outcome and are never able to see the other side of the coin. Your mind is conditioned to see the dark and bleak side of things only.

Say you are about to apply for a new position at work. You've been working hard, and you think you are ready to handle the additional responsibilities that come with this promotion. But right before you go to submit your application, you have a little thought. It sits in the back of your mind, stewing like a roast in a slow cooker: "I don't think I 'm good enough."

It seems harmless, but it makes you hesitate. Why would you think that? You start mulling over all your past achievements. You think through the months you've spent working at this job. What starts as thoughts about your accomplishments quickly slides into thoughts about your failures. You remember that one time you missed an important deadline. You think back to a mistake that made your boss reprimand you. Every word they said floats through your head, a lazy river of doubt. Now, you are focusing on your mistakes, your failures, times when you could have done better. Why did you think you could apply for this job? You barely qualify for the one you had. It's getting harder and harder to remember the good you've done—the bad is so much louder. Just one negative thought was enough to send you into a spiral of self-doubt. You decide not to apply for the position. It should go to someone who deserves it, and that's certainly not you.

Even if you haven't experienced this exact example, you are probably familiar with the self-doubt that comes from these negative thoughts. Maybe you missed a social event, stopped yourself from asking out your crush, or avoided taking a class that seemed too hard. Whatever the specifics, I'm sure you've withheld opportunities from yourself just because of your mindset. I used to do that all the time. Negative thoughts can stop you in your tracks, causing you to miss out on beneficial opportunities, whether you notice you're doing this or not.

On the other hand, by adopting a positive attitude and mindset, you are able to become more open to things. Instead of becoming restricted to doing a certain act, you start considering different ideas and are able to see various possibilities in life. It doesn't even have to be overconfidence or pride; positive thinking simply grants you a path that was previously closed. Instead of revolving around the thought, "I don't think I'm good enough," you can dwell upon the thought, "I'm probably good enough." This very small shift seems inconsequential. What it's really doing is transforming self-doubt into humility. It's ok to not be good at everything, and thinking you are good at everything just sets yourself up for failure. But humility lets you recognize that you can't achieve your goals 100% of the time, and it also lets you believe that most times, you can.

This fact was concluded by a research conducted by Barbara Fredrickson who is a psychology researcher working at the University of North Carolina. To test the influence of different positive emotions and feelings on the human brain, she invited some participants and divided them into five groups. The first and second groups were shown different clips showing positive emotions. The first group saw clips containing joy while the second one saw clips based on contentment. The third group was labelled as the 'control' group and was shown neutral images. The fourth group saw images based on fear, while the fifth one saw images based on anger. Later on, every participant was requested to share their feelings regarding what they would have done in situations shown in the images. Participants of the first groups wrote several possibilities and actions, whereas the ones belonging to the neutral group wrote fewer possibilities and the ones from the fourth and fifth group jotted down only a couple of actions.

This clearly exhibits that positive emotions and thinking help you see different options in a situation to resolve it in the best possible manner, whereas a negative mindset limits your actions and thinking capabilities as well.

Builds Your Skills

With your thinking hindered by negative emotions, you may have certain skills you've never even imagined. If you have trouble convincing yourself that you're good at what you currently do, how could you even begin to explore new areas of expertise? Negative thinking doesn't just hinder your actions, it stops you from thinking of new ones.

Positive thinking empowers you by building your unique skill set. Each one of us is gifted in our own special way. Similarly, you too have some amazing hidden talents, but you are unaware of them. Why? Well, this is simply because you never explored them due to your negative mindset. This is why you are stuck in a terrible job or dependent on others for financial support because you do not bother finding out if you have an extraordinary talent.

However, by developing positive thinking, you become open to the thought that there might be something special about you as well. You might have a talent that could be polished to turn into an amazing skill that could assist you in actualizing all that you have dreamt. This thinking boosts your self-confidence, making you dig deeper in yourself to find out your potential and what you are good at. And once you do that, you can refine your raw talents and enhance them to make them help you achieve all your goals. This frees you from being co-dependent on others and from doing things that you do not enjoy and love.

Positive thinking will also help you with your older talents and passions. Think of a hobby you do have, one that you like and engage in regularly. Imagine if you could engage with that skill completely free from negative thinking. You would be free from doubt, worry, embarrassment, and comparing yourself to others. It would just be you, your skill, and optimism.

Imagine how much more fruitful your work would be if you stopped using these artificial barriers. You would be free to completely explore your talents. Imagine that you want to be a painter. You have some skills, you took a class or two in high school, and you have supplies. Whenever you have the time, you like to sit down and follow an art tutorial or a Bob Ross episode. But you never feel like you're really a painter. You tell people you like to paint, but none of your paintings are on your walls. You don't take pictures of them. You don't show them off or let anyone see you paint. Whether you've noticed it or not, your negative thoughts are making you feel ashamed of a talent you have. If you were free from your negative thoughts, you would be able to talk about painting comfortably, show your work to others, and even talk to other painters about your craft. There is a whole world of painters out there ready to embrace you, and the only thing keeping you from joining them is your thoughts. When you learn to have a positive mindset, you gain the freedom to enjoy the things you spend time on. You don't have to be the next Van Gogh. You don't have to sell your work. You just need to enjoy yourself. And if you're hiding a talent away, you aren't truly enjoying yourself. You aren't truly free. Imagine how much better you'll be when you believe in yourself.

When you first start eliminating your negative thinking from your thought patterns, you might notice you want to explore new areas. Maybe a new craft or trade is more than just a little interesting. Maybe you want to learn to play an instrument, or sew, or start woodworking. You'll begin to discover these new interests as you let yourself think positively about your skills. One thing I noticed, however, when I started this journey, was that my negative thought patterns were not as easy to get rid of just because I was trying new things. For example, I wanted to learn how to work with wood. I went to my local orange hardware store, bought some power tools and 2x4s, and set out to make a small bookshelf. It looked easy enough. Just a few horizontal pieces, a couple vertical pieces, and some wood stain to finish. That bookshelf was horrible. It was ugly, uneven, and it couldn't even hold the weight of my books. I felt like a failure. If I couldn't make something as simple as a bookshelf, how could I possibly make anything else? I stopped woodworking for a long time. I chalked it up to just not having the knack for it, and I looked for hobbies elsewhere. As I continued in my positive mindset journey, I realized how foolish that decision was. How could I possibly expect my first try at a trade to be perfect? With no lessons, no guidance from others, just some tools I didn't know how to use and a picture in my head. I realized that my negative mindset was there that day, telling me that I wasn't good at woodworking. Of course I wasn't! I was a beginner! There's nothing wrong with being a beginner. Practice makes perfect, and with no practice, perfection is impossible.

I like to tell this story because it has a simple and powerful reminder. Your positive mindset journey will be long and inconsistent. It will have ups and downs. The added skills that you gain when you stop limiting yourself will reveal even more opportunities for negative thoughts that you need to discover. As you begin this journey, I urge you to pay attention. You are going to learn to do wonderful things, but if you don't learn to forgive yourself, your journey to a positive mindset will be uneventfully short. In future chapters, you'll learn how to mitigate this effect.

If you want to become empowered in these three amazing ways and want to live a free, happy life full of possibilities, then you must focus on developing an optimistic mindset. How do you develop your positive mindset? You've had your negative one for decades at this point. Let us move on to the next chapter to find out the first step of accomplishing this goal.

# **FREE bonus reminder claim now!**

Chapter 2: How to Develop a Positive Mindset: Understanding that you Possess The Ultimate Power Over Yourself

'I can't change the direction of the wind, but I can adjust my sails to always reach my destination. "Jimmy Dean"

This meaningful quote is a very good example that shows the kind of power that you have over yourself. Examine the quote carefully. What is your understanding of it? If you focus on every word of the quote, you will grasp its true meaning, which clearly states that it is you, who has the ultimate power over yourself and it is you alone who decides whether or not you can reach your set direction. Yes, you cannot change how the wind moves and you cannot force it to move in the direction that benefits you. There are many things that you cannot control, but the good news is, you still have power over the situation. What can you do to improve the situation? You can adjust your sails accordingly so they favor you in moving closer to your destination. Similarly, you cannot stop different obstacles from coming your way, but you can make yourself strong enough to battle any problem that you face and overcome them for good. This idea might sound a bit intimidating and difficult for many, but it is something that everyone is capable of.

I learned to adjust my sails when I was at my first job out of college. I had just spent four years studying political science, and then, after months of applying to every government position I could think of, ended up working sales at a local business. This wasn't what I wanted at all! I was upset. I would go into work every day stressed and sad, feeling like I had lost a game I hadn't realized I was playing. I was convinced that I would never get a job in my desired field. If no one would hire me, was I stuck making cold calls for the rest of my professional life? I wasn't happy at that job, and my performance reflected that. One day my manager called me into his office to discuss my low sales numbers. He told me this Jimmy Dean quote. He said that I was too young to be thinking about my life-long career, that I had so many years ahead of me. The stress I was putting on myself was way too much. He told me that no matter what direction the wind blew, if I was determined enough, I would lead my ship where I wanted. I took that advice to heart. I started to come to work determined, not depressed. I made a true effort, and by the end of the next quarter, I was one of the top salesmen in the office. I got promoted to my manager's position when he moved up, and all of a sudden I wasn't working in sales, I was working in management. I learned how to direct a team, encourage cooperation, and improved my interpersonal skills. I also learned how to hire employees and what recruiters want to see when they interview candidates. With this new knowledge, I went back to apply for those government positions I still dreamed about. This time, I was armed with the experience and knowledge to actually qualify for the jobs I wanted, and I got hired faster than I could have ever imagined. I weathered a storm, turned my sails, and came out on the other side better than my wildest dreams.

While it may sound impossible to turn your sails each and every time the wind blows, you can learn how to do it. If you figure out that you have the power to get through every difficulty in the world, then this should not be impossible for you. Here's how you can do that.

Understand the Power of Your Subconscious

In order to fully understand your subconscious, you must first learn more about how the mind works. Your mind is broadly divided into two main parts: conscious and subconscious minds. The conscious mind is the alert one of the two. This part is what you use for most of your actions while you are awake. You create thoughts, make decisions and perform daily functions with the conscious mind. It knows what's going on and makes you aware of different things happening around you. In addition to that, it orders your subconscious to act in a specific way. Because you know what the conscious mind can do, it is easy to believe that this is the more superior part of your mind when in reality, the subconscious mind is the real player.

Take, for example, making a simple decision, where do you want to go to eat for dinner? Your conscious mind will run down all the different options you have. You could stay home, you could have some Indian food or Chinese, or you could order pizza. As you consider where to go, your subconscious mind is already beginning to make your decision for you. When you think of staying home, you may briefly feel tired. Your subconscious is telling you that you're too tired to cook for yourself. Consciously, if you realize that is what happened, you can now eliminate staying at home from the list of options. When you think of pizza, you feel briefly sick. Your subconscious has a memory that you aren't consciously thinking of. When you try to remember, you recall that you once ate too much pizza in one sitting and got a stomach ache. Now you can consciously decide whether you want to risk having pizza again. You continue this process until you have narrowed down where you want to eat. In this way, your conscious mind is having a conversation with your subconscious. Your subconscious feels, and your conscious thinks.

Your true and special power lies deep in your subconscious. Because this part of the mind remains largely untapped, a lot of people think that it is inactive or perhaps not as functional as the conscious mind. While your conscious mind takes care of all the visible thoughts, emotions, behaviours and activities, your subconscious is in charge of storing all your memories, past feelings, emotions, and thoughts. Each thought that ever formed inside your mind is safely stored in the subconscious and it re-emerges whenever you perceive a similar stimulus. If you use the information locked inside the subconscious in the right manner, you would be able to erase all the bad memories, strengthen your good feelings and thoughts, and enhance your potential. Your subconscious is like a secret trove that has the ability to influence your decisions and actions, but you need to be wise in using it. If you guide it in a positive direction, then it will help you get what you want. However, if you allow your subconscious to be filled with negativity and other dangerous ideas, then it will create a lot of roadblocks ahead and ultimately work against you.

This may seem too good to be true. How could you have a subset of your mind that can change the fundamental way you think? Our brains need to be able to manage different processes without us thinking about it. There are things we need to be in control of, and things that would kill us if we forgot to control them. For example, you can tell the muscles in your fingers and arms to move, but can you tell your heart to beat? Can you tell your stomach to stop digesting? No, and for good reason. If you forgot to think about these things, your physical health would rapidly decline. Imagine if you had a heart attack every time you got distracted by something. Breathing is also something we do automatically, but you can control your breath as well. Just bringing it to mind probably made you take a deep breath just now. Your subconscious is similar to these automatic muscle movements. If you had to concentrate every time you needed to form a memory or feel an emotion, it would be incredibly difficult to navigate the world. Your subconscious takes care of these things for you, so you can focus on other things that require active attention. But, just like your lungs, your subconscious can be influenced by your conscious thoughts and vice versa.

For example, what happens when you always tell yourself that you aren't capable of becoming a good doctor? Your thoughts become infected with this notion and soon enough, you consciously start doing things that prove you can never become an established doctor. This idea will be reflected in most of your actions. The subconscious has the power of framing your emotions, thoughts, and feelings in the exact manner you suggest it to be. A single thought can have a great and lasting effect. What you constantly think about eventually becomes what you are.

Similarly, if you keep appreciating yourself and confidently affirming yourself that nothing could stop you from becoming an excellent doctor, then this positive thinking would make your subconscious believe that you have full potential of achieving your goals. Constant positive thinking will lead you to believe that you would eventually accomplish them. When you exercise control over your thoughts, you will be able to program it in any which way you want. Think of it as a machine that is fuelled by the thoughts and energy that you put in it.

This just proves that your subconscious is an extremely strong and indispensable part of your mind. Many people miss out on its full potential mainly due to a lack of knowledge on how vital it is in changing their lives. Becoming truly powerful begins when you learn how to unleash the full abilities of your subconscious. It is your authentic, special power that will allow you to maximize your potential and do countless things that you never thought you could do.

How can you tell when something you feel or think comes from your conscious or your subconscious? At first, this will be challenging. You are probably used to only thinking of your mind as conscious, so any thoughts you have must come from conscious efforts. Now, you know this isn't true. The difference lies in your self-awareness skills. It takes a long time to develop these skills. You'll need tons of practice, trial and error, and some luck in the beginning. A simple trick I love is to ask myself, "Where did that come from?" If I can answer, then I ask it again. A question chain forms, and eventually it leads to the subconscious idea that started the whole chain in the first place.

For example, I'll notice that I am growing more and more frustrated while out on an errand with my friend. We'll be walking through a grocery store and I get mad when they stand too close, or breathe too loud, or talk to me too much. "This is ridiculous," I'll think, "Why am I mad at my friend for just existing?" So I ask myself that question: "Where is this feeling coming from?" I realize it's coming from a generalized sense of frustration. Well, where is that from? Why am I feeling frustrated? It seems like my patience is lower than normal. Well, why is my patience lower than normal? Where is that from? I then remember that sometimes, usually in late afternoon, I tend to get cranky and short-tempered. Where did that pattern come from? Is it late afternoon? So I check the time and realize it's actually early evening. I've usually eaten dinner by now. "Oh!" I now think. I'm just hangry. So I suggest to my friend that we stop for a bite to eat, and the feelings of frustration disappear. By digging down, I can find the subconscious cause of my conscious emotions.

If you experience an emotion that you can't immediately find a reason for, you're experiencing a conscious emotion caused by subconscious ideas. So how do you go from the bottom up? How do you manipulate your subconscious so that you never have these detrimental thoughts and emotions in the first place?

Unlocking the Potential of Your Subconscious

It may seem counterintuitive that you can manipulate your subconscious. The name "subconscious" itself implies that it is something impossible to think about and that you are always unaware of it. This is true. When you manipulate your subconscious, what you are really doing is establishing a habit of thinking so firmly that it moves from your conscious to your subconscious. It's muscle memory for your thoughts. When you were younger, you had to learn to do a lot of things that are second nature to you now. You learned how to tie your shoes, for example. Now, you've done that simple action so much that you don't need to think about it while you do it. It's like your hands are tying your shoes for you. That is muscle memory at work. Harnessing your subconscious means establishing that same muscle memory for your brain.

Why do so few people unlock their subconscious? Part of it is because people simply aren't taught about it. But mostly, people just don't realize they have subconscious thoughts that influence them. Did you? It's hard to notice the things that we can't think about. Your subconscious influences so much more than you could ever realize, but you probably haven't even realized it exists. You interact with it constantly, however, whether you are aware of it or not. One way you interact with your subconscious is with dreams. Unless you know how to lucid dream, your dreams are controlled by your subconscious. They're the mind's way of processing the events of the day and turning them into memories. Even if you don't remember your dreams, you very likely still have them. Your subconscious helps you store memories so that when you need to, you can recall them. Another way you interact with your subconscious is when you experience something familiar and attach memory to it. For example, when a certain smell reminds you of a place, or when listening to a song makes you remember where you first heard it, your subconscious is the one making these connections and keeping them stored.

You can use these little reminders to help you practice recognizing your subconscious. The more you practice, the easier it will be to realize why you feel certain emotions or remember certain things. As you learn to identify what your subconscious does, you'll discover the inner workings of your own thoughts. This will make unlocking your potential much easier. It's giving yourself the key to your thoughts. Even though you can't directly access your subconscious, recognizing it will let you guide how it flows. Think of your subconscious like a dog or cat. You can't talk to your dog, but as you get to know it, you can learn to recognize its body language and interpret what it wants.

Now that you are becoming more aware that your subconscious has unimaginable power that can be harnessed to your advantage, you need to work on some techniques that will enable you to release that power. But before you proceed, there is one thing that you need to do first. You need to believe that you can be free and powerful. How can you do that? Start with this simple trick that everyone can do.

Simple Practice

Believing in the power of your subconscious mind may prove to be quite challenging especially if you are not at all familiar with this practice. Before today, you didn't even bother crediting your subconscious with some power, let alone believing it. Therefore, you won't be able to place all your faith in it effectively right away. However, a small and helpful practice can make this exercise easier.

Begin by telling yourself, 'I believe in the power of my subconscious mind and I am going to completely harness it.' Repeat this to yourself aloud about 20 times. Yes, it is important that you say it at least 20 times. Once you are finished repeating this positive suggestion 20 times, take note of the feeling brimming inside you. Be conscious of your inner emotion. Is it a positive one? Does it make you feel a tad bit confident about yourself? If yes, then that suggestion has certainly worked its magic. To believe in your subconscious mind's powerful and limitless ability, you need to tell yourself that these powers indeed exist. You need to acknowledge that your subconscious can help bring you closer to what you want to achieve. Repeatedly speaking about it will soon make you trust this suggestion. It is a simple but effective way to channel positivity and to transform your thoughts and actions. By starting with this habit, you are now on the path of taking full control of your subconscious.

What this practice will do is slowly teach you to be aware of your subconscious. As you practice it, you'll discover how much easier it is to notice when your subconscious is telling you something. When you get a new car, you immediately notice that that same model is on the road all around you much more frequently than normal. Did everyone buy that car at the same time you did? Of course not! You added that model to your subconscious and now you notice it when you see it. Before your purchase, the car was not significant to you, so you never gave it a second glance. When you go through this exercise, you are recreating this effect in your mind. Noticing your subconscious deliberately will put it on your radar, just like buying that car. Now, when your subconscious tells you something, you'll have primed your brain to alert you. Repeating to yourself that you have power over your subconscious makes you more ready to embrace that power. So instead of experiencing an emotion or memory without any clue as to why, you'll have primed yourself to address these things.

As we delve deeper into understanding the subconscious, we will talk about essential techniques that you need to be familiar with. These include using positive affirmations, becoming mindful, developing a positive thinking pattern, using NLP techniques and finding good in bad situations. These will all be discussed in detail in the following chapters. It's important to remember that developing mindfulness is both active and passive. The passive parts are things such as reading this book, in which you are training your subconscious to passively be more positive. Active changes, such as the practice listed here and in other chapters, require you to do them with as much dedication as you can muster. It may seem like passive changes are easier, but they won't happen at all if you aren't making active changes to your life. Many people starting their self-improvement journeys fail to realize this and struggle to continue, thinking that they can't improve or are using the wrong methods. If you put in effort to actively make changes, you will see changes. Make sure you keep that in mind as we move on to the next chapters.

Chapter 3: Develop a Positive Thought Process

Shoes were squeaking against waxed wooden floors. The sound of rubber hitting the ground echoed off the walls, and a boy sat on the sidelines, head in his hands, bouncing his leg up and down without even thinking about it. The boy, the newest recruit for the local high school's basketball team, was about to face a terrible fear: playing in front of the whole school for the very first time.

The nerves were making him shake, and his hands slipped through his hair repeatedly as he listened to his teammates warm up. Why did he feel like this? He's practiced every day, nd they play scrimmages against this team regularly. He's played in smaller intramural clubs before and he was never this nervous. Why did he all of a sudden feel sick to his stomach?

As his coach drilled the other players, the boy watched them dribble and practice shooting free-throws. He couldn't help but worry that he'll cause them all to go home disappointed tonight. What if he misses the first shot he takes? They'll never pass to him again! That would be so humiliating. Maybe, he could choke on the first game, and then the coach would never play him again. At least then he would only have to embarrass himself once. He'd need to find an entirely new hobby after that though, another passion besides basketball. How boring that would be. For the boy, there was nothing quite like the thrill of the court that truly brought him joy.

So, what should he do? As he sat on the bench, agonizing over his incoming defeat, another teammate walked up to him, sipping on some water. This was one of the older players, a junior. He had an entire season under his belt. The boy looked away as his teammate approached.

"Hey, man," the older student said, "You're not warming up? Did you hurt your leg or something?"

"Maybe," said the boy, "my stomach really hurts, I don't think I can play tonight."

The junior sat next to the boy as he drank. "You know," he said, watching the other players on the court, "I felt like that at my first game, too."

The boy looked up at the older student, wondering how he could have read his mind so perfectly. "What did you do?" he asked.

"It's kinda simple, once you think about it," the junior turned to look at the boy, "you just have to tell yourself that you're the best player out there."

"What?!" the boy was shocked. "That's a lie!"

"Maybe, but after a while, it will start to feel true. And anyway, who's actually the 'best' is completely made-up, ask any of these guys and they'd all have a different answer. If you get on that court thinking you're the best, you'll sure play like it."

The coach gestured to the bench, calling both players back to the warm-up. The boy stepped onto the court, the stomach ache he'd had before fading. He took his teammate's advice. That night, he didn't score the most points, or catch any rebounds, or even play past halftime. But now it didn't matter. He was the best player out there, no matter what.

From reading the last chapter, you now know why it's so important to have positive thoughts. You also know that those thoughts start from your subconscious. How do you retrain your subconscious to think positive things? By deliberately thinking positive until it's such an ingrained habit that you do it without thinking consciously about it.

At this point, you are most likely determined to liberate your mind from any limitations that keep you from attaining everything you have ever wanted. You know well that this is possible with the help of your subconscious. The first step to accomplishing this goal is to develop a positive thought process. A positive thought process refers to having a healthy, optimistic thinking pattern wherein you think assuredly about everything that is going to happen to you or is happening with you.

For instance, if you were to participate in a debate competition and have a positive thought process, you wouldn't think that you would lose. Instead, you would choose to feel confident that you would be declared as a winner. And even if you did not win, you would feel that you gained a lot from participating in the said event. Hence, a positive thought process enhances your thinking pattern. It helps you focus on the positive and productive and shut out the negative and unrewarding. Once you develop this ability, you will acquire complete freedom from negative thoughts. You will never be bothered by such ideas again.

In order to start forming a positive thought process, you need to learn how to identify and quash your negative thoughts. If you can't tell a positive thought from a negative or neutral one, how can you expect to change your thoughts at all? Once you develop better awareness of your thoughts, you can start shifting thoughts from negative to positive. Once you feel comfortable shifting your negative thoughts, you can focus on adding positive ones to your day. And, if it's hard to add positive thoughts directly, you can at least learn how to give yourself the benefit of the doubt. Let us look at the things you need to do to gain a better thought process and change it from an unconstructive one to an optimistic one.

Step 1 - Identifying the Negative Thought Patterns

First and most importantly, you need to identify what sort of negative thoughts usually form in your mind. If you can identify which type of thought you have, it will be much easier to remember the solution to that thought. These negative thought patterns commonly occur and are experienced by many:

• Catastrophizing: When you think that a bad situation is going to end up far worse than it actually is, you are catastrophizing. In a way, you are blowing things out of proportion. For instance, if you become feverish, you immediately think you are going to die. This can also occur in more subtle ways, such as worrying you'll get fired from your job for making one mistake. The danger in catastrophizing is that it causes you a lot of unnecessary stress and anxiety. If you find yourself immediately jumping to the worst-case scenario every time something less than ideal happens, you're probably catastrophizing.

• Mind Reading: You think you know exactly what other people are thinking. For instance, if you always assume that your boss hates you, then you will end up believing that you will never get that promotion. Mind reading is common in social situations. People tend to believe that others think just like they do. If you are anxious about a task, you assume that all your co-workers are, too. Usually, this habit can lead to social anxieties and trouble talking to authority figures. When you find yourself trying to predict the thoughts and reactions of others, you're probably using this negative thinking pattern instead.

- Over-generalizing: This refers to making a decision based on just one incident. For instance, if you forgot to include an important report in a presentation, you'd say, 'I always forget to do this.' even if it only occurred once. It's incredibly easy to over-generalize. People tend to perceive negative events more than positive ones, and they remember bad things better than good things. When you over-generalize, you end up amplifying this effect, making you much more pessimistic than you should be. This is why keeping a journal and writing things down is so important. Your written record will disprove many of the over-generalizing thoughts that run through your head.

- Black and White Thinking: This means that you think that a certain scenario can only have either a bad or a good outcome, and that there can't be any middle way. For instance, you may think 'He is the best or the worst.' Because of black and white thinking, you won't probably consider that 'He has his flaws, but he is a decent man.' Black and white thinking is one of the most common negative thought processes experienced. This is mostly because it's the most normalized. Movies, TV shows, and most other media instill in us the idea that things are only good or bad, not in between. It can be difficult to break this pattern, but until you do, your thoughts will be much more bitter than necessary. Try to consider events in your day-to-day life from both sides. How did you react to that situation, but also how do you think the other people involved reacted? Your guess may not be completely true, but just in asking the question, you let yourself think in grays.

- Critical Self-Talk: It refers to having a negative image of yourself. You constantly tell yourself that you can't do something, or highlight your flaws and mistakes. For instance, always thinking that 'I am a loser' or 'I am a failure.' Remember from chapter one that criticizing yourself and being humble are two very different things. You don't need to constantly berate yourself, that's not constructive. Your critical self-talk can lead to low self-esteem issues very quickly. If you have trouble controlling these thoughts, try to replace them with temporary things. Instead of "I can never give good presentations" think, "That presentation I gave today could have been better".

- Predicting your Future: You believe that you know exactly how things are going to turn out. For instance, you think that you will definitely fail a test even before you actually take it. This one is especially common if you are prone to anxious thoughts. These thoughts tend to set us up for failure before we even give ourselves a chance. Predicting your future is not the same as making plans. Making a plan implies control over a situation. When you predict the future, you make assumptions based on the idea that you have no control of the situation at all. If you're regularly falling into this thought pattern, you're probably a very anxious person. As you develop self-awareness, it will get easier for you to identify this thought pattern, and you can start working to stop it.

Which of these do you normally experience? It is important to find out which negative thinking pattern is affecting your mindset. Keeping a log or a journal will help you become more aware of determining this. Whenever a negative thought pops in your mind, jot it down in the journal along with the time, date and incident related to that thought. Figure out to which category it belongs, in order to keep track of your current thought process.

When you start your journal, it will be difficult to identify negative thoughts, let alone to categorize them. During your first few days, or even weeks, you should focus on simply writing down your thoughts. If you have a thought that is particularly emotional, write it down and record how it made you feel. Over time, you will be able to readily recognize whether a thought is negative or positive. Then, you can just write down the negative ones and practice identifying which category your thought belongs to. This list of thought types is extensive but not comprehensive. Do some research on your own to find out what kind of thoughts you have. If you have a type of thought you have trouble categorizing, make your own category for it. Everyone is different and thinks in different ways, so don't feel defeated if some of your thoughts don't match these categories. In fact, you should feel proud. Noticing that a thought is outside of any of these categories indicates that you have a very deep understanding of the thoughts that do belong in these categories. It also means you have a very keen ability to recognize your own thoughts and trace them back to their subconscious roots. The more you practice writing this down, the better you will get at identifying and categorizing your thoughts.

Identifying your thoughts, however, is only half of the puzzle. It gives you information about yourself, but that information requires action. Once you are able to readily identify what kind of negative thoughts you are having, you can then start to replace those negative thoughts with positive ones.

Step 2 - Replacing Negative Words with Positive Ones

The second step in developing a positive thought process is to slowly eliminate negative words from your routine speech. Gradually get rid of negative thinking by adding more simple and positive words to your speech. For instance, words like 'always', 'must', 'should', 'won't' and 'cannot' and phrases like 'I am sure', 'I already know', add a more decisive tone to your talk including the negative thought. These words trap you. If you're thinking "I can never be a good painter," then you are forcing yourself to make a wrong assertion. It's lying to yourself. You can replace the decisive word with a gentle, open-minded word. "I can never be a good painter" becomes "I can develop my skills to become a good painter." Give yourself room for improvement.

To start, you can replace these words with neutral words if positive ones are too difficult. Add a word that brings doubt to your negative thought, such as "might" or "think." Self-doubt is usually something to be avoided, but here you are using it constructively. You are adding doubt to a negative thought, and therefore increasing your confidence just by adding a word. Now, your thought becomes "I might never be a good painter." All of a sudden, you have given yourself room to grow. Your negative thoughts are constantly bombarding you, making you doubt yourself and your abilities. With this technique, you are using this tool against your thoughts. In essence, you are learning to use a double negative to make a positive. Not everyone who is on their mindset journey needs this approach—some can start with positive words right off the bat. But for others, it can feel like lying to yourself when you replace the negative words with purely positive ones. For example, say you are insecure about your public speaking abilities. For years, you think, "I am a terrible public speaker." Switching to "I am a great public speaker," even when it's true, can be more upsetting than it is helpful. It feels like lying to yourself, even like you're making fun of yourself. The neutral language will help you bridge this gap. With neutral language, you can think, "I am not the worst public speaker out there," or, "If I practice, I will get better at public speaking." Once you get used to these thoughts, you can start thinking positive ones. Most of the time, the positive thoughts are actually true, but if they feel like a lie, take it slow.

What kind of words do you usually tell yourself? Are they helpful, or do they make you feel burdened? Observe how your daily thoughts affect you. When you say things like, 'I always make so many mistakes' or 'I cannot get anything done', you assure yourself that you are never going to improve. By saying negative things such as, 'I am sure I am going to fail' or 'I am never going to pass the test', you let yourself believe that you are incapable of doing something. Words and thoughts like these can easily plague your mind and infiltrate your thought process. Therefore, these words need to be eliminated from your mind and from your speech. Jot down all the negative words you commonly use in your 'thought journal' and find positive replacements for them. Now, you can replace words before you think them.

Study your list of negative words thoroughly, and memorize their positive counterparts. If you need to use flashcards, do so. Try to have your list with you at all times until you memorize it so you can always look back on it. Whenever you catch yourself thinking a negative word, quickly replace it with the positive word you've pre-prepared. The faster you can do this, the better. For instance, replace 'cannot' with 'can' and 'won't' with 'will.' Instead of thinking 'I cannot do it', tell yourself 'I can try' or 'I can do it.' By adding positive words and phrases to your speech, you will feel that your thoughts are slowly becoming more positive as well. As you get more and more practice with this, you'll find that it becomes easier to replace these words. You'll find yourself reacting without thinking about it, catching yourself saying a negative word as though you're swearing somewhere you shouldn't be. Eventually, you'll stop thinking the negative words altogether. It will become such a habit to correct yourself that you'll change your thought patterns permanently. Just like speaking another language, you'll be able to move through your day with your thoughts submerged in these positive words. You will have full freedom from your negative thoughts.

But freedom from negative thoughts is only the second step. You can also learn to actively think positively in places where you normally wouldn't have charged thoughts at all. Positive self-talk will lead you to a true mindset shift.

Step 3 - Practice Positive Self-Talk

Positive self-talk or positive affirmation refers to saying affirmative things to yourself. It is the best tactic to get rid of the catastrophic, over-generalizing, mind reading, future predicting and critical self-talk practices your mind tends to fall into. In positive self-talk, you constantly tell yourself good and productive things to make your subconscious believe that you have what it takes to achieve something. Whenever a negative thought pops in your mind, you quickly replace it with a positive affirmation. Always be ready to transform any negative idea into a positive thought. Make yourself familiar with affirmative phrases, and always keep them in mind. For instance, 'I am sure I'm going to fail' should be replaced with 'I am going to pass' and 'I always err' needs to be converted to 'I am going to do it right.' When you find yourself thinking 'I am not good enough for this job', you can tell yourself 'I may not be the best at this job, but I will learn and improve.'

Positive self-talk is a step beyond simply replacing negative thoughts with positive ones. You aren't just putting a bandage on a wound, you're taking an antibiotic so it never has a chance to get infected. You're boosting your confidence, improving your self-esteem. When you practice positive self-talk, you actively take power away from your negative thoughts. Think about it: If you dedicate time in your day to telling yourself you are good at things, then when your subconscious tries to tell you you're bad at something, it's incredibly obvious how wrong that is. Your positive self-talk is a built-in lie detector. The more you practice using it, the stronger your detector will become.

This goes a step further than replacing words because it isn't simply filling in gaps. In a sinking ship, it's important to stop up any leaks, but eventually you have to get to land and build a better ship. Positive self-talk is building your better ship. Before, you were going about your day thinking negatively about yourself. With hard work, you fixed that and turned your negative thoughts into positive ones. But you only changed the thoughts you had into better ones. You didn't invent new thoughts. You didn't make room for new, better thoughts to flourish. Now, you can. Your positive self-talk should be in addition to your other thoughts throughout the day. I like to start my day with some positive affirmations, simple things to encourage myself when I wake up. You can put them on sticky notes on your bathroom mirror, or set them as a reminder on your phone so you see them throughout the day. The more you think these thoughts, the more positive your mindset will become. You'll bring optimism into your day-to-day life. Replacing your negative words with positive ones was like smoothing a path in the forest, instead of hiking through bare wilderness. With your positive self-talk, you're paving that path and strapping on some roller skates, flying down the path and having fun while you go. It's taking your mindset to the next level.

On the other hand, be careful with using words and phrases such as always, I'm sure, I already know, must and should to your affirmation because these words burden you. It is best to steer clear of those. These words make you feel that you need to do something a certain way and when that happens, you start doubting yourself. For instance, by saying, 'I'm sure I am going to pass', you are burdened with the responsibility of passing the exam and in case that doesn't happen, you will start losing yourself to negative thinking once again. Instead of encouraging you, it will cause you to become too hard on yourself. This is exactly why these words must be avoided at all times.

Mindfulness is all about balance. You can't be too negative on yourself, or you will risk deflating your sense of self-worth. On the other hand, if you fall into toxic positivity, you can risk severely hindering yourself. When you learn to replace your negative words with positive ones, you will often find yourself replacing definitive words with open-ended words. You can apply this to positive self-talk as well. Don't paint yourself into a corner, negatively or positively. One of the best ways to prevent this is by practicing forgiveness. Your journey to positive thinking will not be a straight line. You will have good and bad days, as all of us do. When you have bad days, it is easy to feel like you have failed. It can feel like you've let yourself down, disappointing yourself because you can't live up to your own expectations. If you are using toxic positivity, like the thought, "I will have a good day," and you leave no room for doubt, then when you fail to meet this impossible standard, you feel discouraged. In this moment, forgiveness is your best tool. Forgive yourself for not always having good days. You are allowed to make mistakes or have temporary lapses in self-control. Real progress is when you notice that these bad days are becoming rarer and rarer as time goes on.

Make a habit of positively affirming yourself in every situation, so that your mind starts accepting these suggestions. It will become easier for you to dismiss any thought that is not helping you. Keep on feeding your mind with positivity, and the negative thoughts will eventually diminish. In about three to four weeks, you will experience a marked improvement in your thinking pattern and will see it slowly changing to a positive one.

Step 4 - Add "Yet" to Your Speech

The fourth thing you need to do is to include the word 'yet' to your speech. This word adds possibility to your speech and gives you the hope that if you aren't able to do something right now, you might be able to learn it in the future. This thinking pattern is also known as the growth mindset, which believes that each person is capable of improving themselves. By accepting that you can grow and become better, you do not restrict yourself to your current state and set of skills. Instead, you focus and work on refining them. This realization imparts you with freedom: freedom to work on yourself, freedom to become better and freedom to enhance your skills and abilities. For instance, if you say 'I cannot paint', you feel that you can never learn to paint. But by saying, 'I cannot paint yet', you get the feeling that you might be able to learn this skill later on.

Adding "yet" to your speech will encourage you to think of your progress as an inconsistent but inevitable path. You can't find a regular sleep schedule yet. You just can't seem to land that job yet. However you incorporate it, "yet" will let you think about the future, always looking to improve. It's a simple and incredibly effective way to reduce your self-effacing thoughts in a subtle fashion that still gives you room to not be perfect. "Yet" is such a good word, it's like magic. If you are struggling to find a way to replace your negative and definitive words in your thoughts, adding "yet" will make it easier to understand how you can improve over time. I used to have trouble falling asleep sometimes. I would think over and over to myself, "I can't sleep," and agonize about how much rest I was going to get that night. I tried replacing negative words, telling myself that "I am having trouble sleeping." This didn't help, it felt just as upsetting. When I tried positive self-talk, all it turned into was promising myself caffeine in the morning. But then I added "yet," so my worried thought became, "I can't sleep yet." Suddenly, these thoughts seemed much less stressful. If I can't sleep yet, I'll just wait until I can. It was liberating. I had given myself the freedom to fall asleep later, with no anxious worrying about sleep quality. Adding "yet" to my anxious thought was like giving myself a hand so I could stand up. It was the help I didn't know I needed.

Don't resign to the fact that you will never be able to do something just because it seems impossible right now. Tell yourself that even though you can do it yet, you still have the chance to do it at a later time.

So, if 'yet' hasn't been a part of your routine speech yet, you should start incorporating it into it from now onwards, so your thought process starts becoming a growth one. Adding "yet" is the next step in building your positive mindset. You learned how to identify the negative thoughts, how to replace them, and how to add positive thoughts to your day. But no one can think positive thoughts all the time. So you add "yet." Now, even when you have a negative thought you just can't get rid of, you can give yourself an avenue to look forward to. I use this strategy more often when I have a self-criticism that is actually true. It's not negative or positive, it's an accurate reflection of my abilities, such as, "I'm not good at making small talk." When I add "yet" to these thoughts, it makes it so I feel open instead of insecure. We all have faults and imperfections. No one is perfect, and expecting yourself to be perfect is deeply harmful. So when you find something you aren't good at, you now have a tool to make sure you stay optimistic. In the face of truth, you can still stand tall, knowing that even if you aren't good at something right now, you can always work on improving.

One thing to keep in mind when you are adding "yet" to your true flaws is that you aren't comparing yourself to others. Everyone is different, and if you walk around trying to assess other people's skills against your own, you'll end up disappointed. So, be cautious and make sure your "yet" thoughts aren't comparative. Don't think, "I'm not as good at piano as she is, yet," or anything else along those lines. What you are really doing is pressuring yourself to constantly compete with others. While competition isn't inherently unhealthy, constant unfriendly competition is harmful to your mindset. Monitor your thoughts to make sure you don't make this mistake.

When you are having worrying, negative thoughts, go through these four steps. Find out which type of thought pattern you are experiencing, replace the negative words with positive ones, encourage yourself with positive self-talk, and add yet to your thoughts. Make sure to practice all these four steps routinely to improve your thought process. Remember, you are in control with what goes on in your head, so choose only what is helpful to you. With the right habits, you will achieve a positive thought process, and a mindset that is insusceptible to negativity.

Chapter 4: Appreciate Yourself

A young woman stands alone on the sidewalk. Rain pours down around her, runs through her hair and soaks her thin jacket. She forgot her umbrella today. As she stands on the sidewalk, waiting for her bus, cars move past her. Their tires splash through puddles like a toddler, drenching her each time they pass by. She stands and waits. The rain is not fun, and she checks her watch regularly, waiting for the bus to arrive. Minutes pass and still, nothing. It's not abnormal for the bus to be late, but it is completely out of the ordinary for it to be raining. Late and raining? She sighs. She shifts her weight from foot to foot, brushing water droplets off of her soaked sleeves. How she wishes she had an umbrella. Being soaked so thoroughly is dreadful. But what else could she do? She forgot her umbrella; she condemned herself to this drenched state. If only she had checked the weather, if only she carried a raincoat, if only she had bought a waterproof jacket instead of this cotton one. If only she had a car, so she could drive home. If only she lived closer, so she could walk. The woman stands, sopping and miserable, scolding herself for all her mistakes.

Then, another woman walks past the first. This woman is hurried, walking with her eyes straight ahead, her heels clicking on the sidewalk. She stops next to the soaked woman, briefly glancing at her before crossing the street. As the second woman crosses, the first watches, wishing she had brought an umbrella of her own, pitying the woman crossing the street for getting wet like her. The second woman reaches the other side of the street, then moves to stand under the awning of the restaurant on the corner. She glances at her watch and looks down the road, frustration in her brow. She is waiting for the bus, too, the first woman realizes. *I didn't even think to take cover!* She thinks. Quickly, the first woman moves to follow the second and stand with her under the awning. The bus arrives soon after, and the first woman is able to finally relax.

This story seems simple, but it has a deeper meaning underneath. The first woman got soaking wet in the rain, but she didn't need to. She could have walked across the street and taken cover. What was the difference between her and the other woman? The second woman was focused on positive thoughts and appreciated herself. She valued her own comfort. The first woman was thinking only about her own mistakes. Her thoughts were as negative and dreary as the rain she was standing in. But the second woman was determined to help herself, so she spotted the shade that the other woman hadn't even thought to look for.

Self-appreciation is the key to improving your mindfulness. It will unlock your ability to value yourself, even if your thoughts are negative. When you are in a bad situation, it can be really difficult to remember to take care of yourself.

When you learn to appreciate yourself, regardless of your situation, it's like you are carrying around your own personal cheerleader. That bully you used to carry turns into your number one fan.

If you have been working on having a positive thought process, then kudos to you! You have really made great improvements to your thinking patterns. Now it is time to do another helpful practice that will be of great help in enhancing the positivity emerging inside you. For this next step, you need to learn how to start appreciating yourself and giving yourself credit for the amazing strengths you possess.

Why Appreciate Yourself?

Do you ever wonder why you are never able to accomplish your goals and achieve the success you have dreamt for? Maybe it is due to your inner critic who is constantly scrutinizing and criticizing your every action. Your inner critic is your shattered and negative inner-self; a voice inside you that only sees your weaknesses and pinpoints them as well. It is this voice you have been listening to for a long time, which is why you doubt yourself and are never able to realize your potential.

It's hard to realize you're even doing this to yourself in the first place. Learning to appreciate yourself is a lot like getting your first pair of glasses. For the longest time, you probably walked around thinking the way you saw things was completely normal. Tree leaves look like blobs unless you're right next to them. Roofs on houses don't have individual shingles, it's all one piece. It's normal to not be able to read street names until you're close enough to touch the sign. But then, you get your glasses, and all of a sudden you can see so many things you didn't think possible. Definition in trees and houses, if you really focus you can even see birds in the branches. So that's what bird watching is! The clarity you gain from learning to appreciate yourself is just like getting your first pair of glasses. You probably weren't even aware that the world around you was blurry. Learning to appreciate yourself is difficult because most people don't even realize they lack self-appreciation.

How do you realize you aren't appreciating yourself? It's a hard thing to admit, especially in a time where self-care is almost over-emphasized in social media. Just taking a bath every once in a while isn't self-appreciation. You know if you practice self-appreciation by your answer to these two questions: Do I do nice things just for myself? Why do I do those things? With these two questions, you will start to recognize if you even show yourself appreciation at all, and if you think you do, the second question will reveal your true motives. Say you appreciate yourself by recognizing a specific talent. This seems like self-appreciation, but is it truly? If it was self-appreciation, then your answer to the second question would be that you recognize this talent because you are comfortable showing yourself compassion and love. If it was not self-appreciation, then your answer would be related to something superficial and materialistic. "I am good at painting because I'm good at making art that looks like a Monet." That's impressive, but it's unfriendly competition and it doesn't give yourself any credit. "I'm good at painting because looking at my work makes me happy." This is true self-appreciation because it focuses on an emotional connection that does not stem from comparing yourself to others or from superficial measurements. If you are mostly thinking like the former, you probably don't have enough appreciation for yourself.

However, by learning to appreciate yourself, you give yourself confidence and the assurance that you aren't useless or hopeless and that you too, have something to be proud of. You may have some weaknesses, but there's something special about you as well. Something that you can be proud of. This gives you the courage to believe in yourself and move forward as a confident individual who isn't restricted by their self-critic and is free to do whatever they please.

We tend to fall into the habit of self-minimization in the attempt to be humble and kind. It's really easy to believe that thinking you are good at something is bad or toxic. This is because we are often raised to think like this. But it's not conceited, it's not prideful, and it definitely isn't attention-seeking to appreciate yourself. Self-appreciation means that you embrace your talents. It means you are able to recognize the things you are good at and forgive yourself for the things you could improve on. It means valuing your own opinions as much as you do others'. As you learn to appreciate yourself, you will find that what you're really learning is how to love yourself.

Everyone is unique, everyone has value, everyone has talents and strengths. It's common for people working on their mindset to already think this. It's easy to recognize the value that others bring to the table, but it's just as easy to forget about your own. When you learn to appreciate yourself, you'll end up ingraining into your mind that you have value, too. This journey will be uncomfortable. It certainly was for me. One of the things I do to make appreciating myself easier is to remind myself of the definition of pride. Pride is thinking you are better than the people around you. It's believing that you are more valuable, talented, smarter or more sophisticated than others you interact with. On the other hand, self-appreciation is believing that you, just like everyone else, have value and contribute meaningfully to the world around you. It is not a bad thing to be appreciative of yourself. It is not conceited or mean. In fact, appreciating yourself often benefits others, because you begin to participate more in the conversations and projects around you. Learning to appreciate yourself is really important in developing your positive mindset. To enjoy the full benefits of a positive mindset, it is essential that you work on praising yourself. Here are a few steps on how you can do that.

Create an Inventory of Your Strengths

There are a few ways you can practice developing your self-appreciation. The first is to make a list. Just like the journal you are keeping to track your negative thoughts, writing down your strengths is a way to make you instantaneously aware of them. It also reminds you on a daily basis of what your strengths are. Having a list is a good way of keeping track of things you want to remember or accomplish. People make lists as a reminder for all sorts of things. Why not make a list of your strengths to remind you that you're good at something?

Take a pencil and a paper and jot down everything nice about you. Don't over think each idea, just write down whatever comes to mind. This list could include the strengths, talents or other good attributes that you think you have. If you are unable to think of any, then try to remember any positive qualities others think you have. For instance, think of the time you helped your father with his business report and he told you that you were good at making reports. Maybe, making good reports is your specialty. You can also think of any similar events and dig deeper into yourself to come up with a list of your strengths. Label this list as your 'strengths inventory.' This list will give you the hope that you aren't a lost cause and that you have a lot of things to be happy about. Always keep it with you and take a look at it from time to time to strengthen the belief that you are an amazing individual with a lot of unique strengths. This will help build and increase your self-confidence.

You should reflect on this list regularly. Don't just write down a characteristic and then forget about it. Start your day by reading through your list of strengths. End your day by asking yourself which of those qualities you utilized. Maybe today you used your empathy to help your friend make a decision. Maybe you used your art skills at work. As you better develop your self-awareness, you'll be able to add more and more talents to your list. Once you have developed your list to a place that you think is robust, start keeping track of when you use your talents as well. This will be the other half of your list. You'll now add your strengths like normal and how you use them throughout your day. When you reflect on your list, you'll be able to see what you are good at and concrete examples of how you have put that into action in the past.

Actions speak much louder than words, and that's true for your self-improvement journey as well. When you see your talents put into action, you'll be able to convince yourself that what you do is important. It will make it much easier to appreciate yourself. For example, one of the first strengths I wrote down for myself was that I was good at cooking. At the time, I cooked a few dinners here and there for my family, and they always liked it, but whenever I talked to people about talents and hobbies, cooking never came up. I put it on my list and started to reflect on it more. I decided to write down my friends and families reviews of my cooking, and wrote them in my journal as though it was a restaurant review column in a newspaper. This forced me to actively think about what people said when they ate my food. The positive reactions were harder to write off when I was writing them down. Their complements were harder to ignore. I soon became much more appreciative of my ability to cook. I didn't let the compliments get to my head, of course—I'm no professional chef. But now, I know that if I bring a homemade dish to a potluck, my friends aren't eating it out of pity, they're eating it because it tastes good. After this experience with journaling, I tell people who ask that one of my hobbies is cooking, because that's the truth. I just didn't appreciate myself enough to recognize it.

You may try to do this task, sitting down with your pen on paper, and realize that you simply can't think of anything. You can't think of a single thing to write. Does that mean you don't have any strengths? Does that mean you are simply average, that you don't have talents worth noting? Absolutely not! Just because you have trouble thinking of your strengths doesn't mean you don't have them. Everyone is unique. We all have unique personalities and capacities. Because of this, everyone in the world has talents they can utilize to become their best selves. Even if you can't see it, you have strengths. So, how do you go about finding what they are? If you can't see your own strengths, that's ok. Your self-esteem may be too low for you to properly evaluate them. That's ok, since you're making an active effort to improve your mindset, it is clear that you have recognized this issue and you are working to fix it. In the meantime, ask your friends and family. If you can, ask your parents what they think your strengths are. Or ask your significant other, or your closest friends. You could even ask your boss, if you want work-related strengths. Write down whatever people tell you. Write it down even if you don't believe them. Write it down even if you can't see in yourself what they see in you. Write it down, read through it, and regularly reflect on the list. The more you read it, the more you will get used to the idea that you have strengths. It will get easier and easier to believe that they are true. Over time, you will come to recognize what other people see in you for yourself. When that happens, you will feel a large boost in your confidence. This boost will then let you continue with your positive mindset journey. You will be free from the insecurities that previously held you back so far. Even if you do have a sizable list of strengths without help, you should ask around to see what others think of you. You never know how you are perceived by others—you can't read minds, after all.

Make Positive Suggestions Using Your List

You can take your journal to the next level by writing in suggestions for yourself. Instead of a simple list with examples, add in words of affirmation to say to yourself that will help you suggest your strengths to yourself throughout your day. Expand your strengths beyond simple words and phrases. For each, write a full sentence that demonstrates the talent you are trying to emphasize, how you use it, and why it's important. Take your list and make suggestions for every strength that you have written down. For instance, if one of your strengths is 'good debater', then make a suggestion stating, 'I am confident and excellent at debating.' Similarly, if you have written, 'kind hearted', you should make a suggestion stating, 'I am a kind person who spreads love.' After the suggestions have been created, you need to make a habit of saying them aloud for about 20 to 30 times daily. The purpose behind creating these positive statements is to strengthen your belief that you have great abilities to be happy for. It will also help you enhance these talents. When you repeatedly say good things to yourself, your mind embraces them and starts creating positive thoughts accordingly. Your positive thoughts then start moving around, attracting positive opportunities and helping you accomplish your set goals. Like what you have learned earlier in this book, positive thinking helps create productive actions.

Your suggestions should be phrases that emphasize your strengths. They should help you conceptualize what these strengths mean, why they are important, and how you can use them in your day-to-day life. Examples of suggestions include: "I am a talented musician," "I am good at communicating with others," "I am a true friend to those around me," or even, "I am good at math." By writing down and repeating your suggestions, you can memorize these wider contexts. Now, when you go about your day, it will be much easier to notice when you are using a certain strength and how that use helped you. For example, say one of your strengths is that you are understanding. You can make a suggestion that says, "When someone in my life has a different experience than me, I can understand them." Now, when you actually go and meet someone who is different from you, you will remember your strength. It will be easier to ask this new person questions about their life and experiences. You'll gain new knowledge of the world and use this knowledge to better understand the people around you, just like your suggestion said you would. When you go back to read your suggestion again, you'll be reminded of that conversation, again embedding in your mind that your strength is understanding. This creates a feedback loop that will teach you that your strengths have an impact on your day-to-day life. It's much easier to appreciate yourself when you learn this.

This step will affirm in your mind that you are capable of these strengths. With that affirmation, you will gain the ability to see your strengths in the context of others. This is where healthy competition comes in. You will not only witness how you use your talents, you will see exactly how your talents affect others in a positive way. Knowledge that you are capable of improving the world around you is the best way to make you feel better about yourself. We grow by helping others. No one sits at home all day, doing nothing, and feels good about themselves. You need social interaction to show yourself your true talents. By making positive suggestions for yourself, you are documenting your ability to help others. Whether this manifests as helping your team, helping a project, helping a friend or loved one, or simply making work move smoothly, when you embrace your talents, you learn to appreciate the difference you make in the world.

When you finally adopt true self-appreciation, your whole world will change. The negative thoughts that you bombard yourself with are relentless in their pursuit to pull you down. Take away their power. Remove them from your life. Appreciate yourself, your strengths, your talents, your habits, your goals, and you'll learn that those negative thoughts are all wrong. It's time to put an end to that constant criticism. Give yourself a much needed pat on your back so you can start feeling good about yourself. When you feel good about yourself, you start behaving accordingly as well. Your mind stops creating negative thought patterns once you make it a habit to focus on your strengths and believe in what you can do.

Do Something Nice for Yourself

After becoming more self-aware of your strengths and creating positive statements, it is important to reward yourself. Learn how to treat yourself to something once in a while. Let's say you passed a difficult test. You can reward yourself by going to a concert during the weekend. It can even be as simple as buying your favourite comfort food, watching a movie or just giving yourself some moments to relax and unwind. Allow yourself to feel good about the things you accomplish. Doing something nice for yourself is a way of reaffirming yourself for your achievements no matter how big or small they are. This will also help you in renewing your energy and perspective so that you will feel more confident in facing the challenges that come.

Self-care is critical to your well-being. True self-care is an expression of the love and appreciation you have for yourself. It isn't simply eating ice cream once a week or going on a shopping spree. Self-care is showing yourself compassion so that you can reset yourself mentally. It's taking a day off of work for your mental health. It's eating a nice meal without thinking about body image. It's buying yourself something you've been wanting for a while but haven't explicitly needed. It can also be routine actions you take to keep yourself healthy. Exercise is self-care; so is eating healthy. Self-care is incredibly helpful for your mental and physical well-being.

To get into the habit of self-care, pick an activity to start out. Try to pick something very easy that doesn't take much time or effort. Exercise is usually not a very good one to start out with if you struggle to do it right now. You can try a nice skincare routine for your mornings. You could take a bath at night to unwind. You could also find a book you want to read and dedicate half an hour a day to reading it. Find a small, easy self-care action and do it every day. After two weeks, if you've done it every day, or at least most days, you can add something a little more complex. Add self-care routines to your day in steps like this, making sure you can maintain them for two weeks at a time so that you can make them a habit. If you try to add something to your day, say, taking a short walk, and you find yourself unable to do it daily, that's ok. For the first three habits, if you struggle to make it daily, don't do it. The first three habits should be very easy to stick to. If it isn't, forgive yourself and try something else. This will ensure that you build and maintain self-confidence while you are making these routines. Your self-confidence will do two things. First, it will improve your overall mindset. Second, it will make adding more complex habits, such as exercise, much easier. Basically, you're getting into the habit of forming habits. Self-care should be a habit for you. By gradually adding it piece by piece, you give yourself an exponentially higher chance of success.

Take Criticism Less Seriously

Appreciating yourself also means knowing how to handle criticism from others. Self-assurance will help you eliminate the burden of always wanting to get approval from others. Seeking validation from others can create unnecessary pressure that may lead to negative and unproductive thinking. Instead, learn how to be confident with your own abilities. Use criticism to improve yourself, but don't let it take total control of your thoughts.

Letting go of criticism is incredibly difficult. We grow up in systems, such as public school, that emphasize criticism of our performances. What are letter grades if not critiques of all our academic work? In the adult world, these critiques can be a lot less concrete, but just as important. How do you go about taking lightly something you've been trained to take very seriously? Unfortunately, it is as hard as it sounds, but with the right mindset and practice, anyone can do it.

First, remind yourself that the vast majority of the time, people aren't actually criticizing you. Think of taking the subway or being on a plane. Are you spending that whole time thinking about other people? Probably not. More likely, you're spending that time using your phone, thinking about plans, or taking a nap. You are paying much more attention to yourself than you are to other people. That's a universal truth. Most people pay more attention to themselves than to others. You don't notice that your co-worker's nose is big, that's just what her face looks like. Even if she is insecure about it, you don't think about it at all. Criticism from others is much less common than it seems. When you are trying to liberate yourself from criticism, the first step is to remember that there is much less criticism in your life than you think.

Second, remember that no one knows one another enough to judge each other completely. Your boss may know you at work, but they probably don't know your personal life very well. Your spouse knows your personal life very well, but might not be familiar with your professional self. Your friends know certain aspects of you that your family doesn't know, and vice versa. No one knows us better than we know ourselves. So, when you do receive criticism, constructive or otherwise, remember that the person criticizing you only has a piece of information about you, never the full picture. No one can know all of the qualities of your personality except you, and unless you have perfect self-awareness, it's hard for you to know all of them, too. The criticism you receive is never complete or total. When you know this, it becomes much easier to receive criticism. That person is not critiquing your whole being, just one small piece of it.

The third and final thing you can do to make sure you take criticism less seriously is to remember that no one is perfect. You aren't perfect, but neither are the people around you. Their thoughts and opinions are shaped by their experiences, moods, and past, just like yours. If someone offers criticism to you, remember that they aren't always right. Sometimes people are just plain wrong about things. If you feel their thoughts are valid, you can have a conversation with them about fixing whatever they are criticising. But if, after reflection, you don't think they are right, then you are perfectly free to take what they say with a grain of salt. It's not prideful; it's simply appreciating your own capacities.

Self-appreciation is a long and complex road, with plenty of bumps along the way. But when you finally gain it, your world will expand. Appreciating yourself will be the greatest gift you've ever received. It gives you the freedom to have confidence. It alleviates negative feelings about yourself. It lets you interact with the world how you want, not how others want. Once you learn to appreciate yourself, you'll find joy in improving your mindset even further. The next step is to grow even more aware of your negative thoughts, getting rid of them once and for all.

Chapter 5: Become Mindful of the Negative Thoughts to Eradicate Them

Mindfulness has lots of different meanings for different people. For those who have a successful mindset, mindfulness means complete understanding of the thoughts, emotions, and subconscious influences that affect their mind. When someone has a true grasp of their own mind, they can start approaching their thoughts not as an involuntarily meandering stream, but as an ocean of knowledge to pull from at will. Mindfulness is imperative for developing a positive mindset. If you don't know why you are thinking and feeling the thoughts that you think and the emotions you feel, then how can you start changing them for the better? Say you are stressed and anxious about an important presentation coming up. You've been preparing all week but that hasn't helped your nerves. Someone without mindfulness might register that the presentation is the cause of their stress, but when that stress causes lack of patience and frustration at home, they won't be able to tell why they are feeling negative emotions. They might not even be able to recognize that they are feeling these emotions in the first place. They may only be able to act upon them. Someone who is practicing mindfulness is able to notice these emotions, figure out that they are caused by stress, locate the source of the stress, and are even able to take steps to mitigate the stress caused by the meeting. For example, they know themselves so well that they know that if they write down a script, they will feel more prepared. Mindfulness leads you to a level of self-control that you likely haven't experienced before. In this chapter, you'll learn to expand your mindfulness skills step by step. If you follow these practices, you'll soon learn how to interpret your thoughts and emotions in any situation.

Let's start this chapter off with a short practice. Set aside five minutes for this. Sit down in a quiet room. Close your eyes and breathe. Breathe steadily, and try to clear your mind of thoughts. What are the thoughts you are trying to clear? Try to notice them, but don't let them become fully fledged ideas. For example, if you think, "I need to sweep the kitchen later," don't think about sweeping the kitchen. Try your hardest to acknowledge that you have a chore and then move on to the next thought. If you have trouble sitting still for this long, put on some relaxing music in the background. As long as it is relaxing and doesn't have lyrics, it will help you concentrate. Set a timer and sit like this for at least five minutes, or as long as you are comfortable. Notice your thoughts and the world around you as you try to steady your breaths. Congratulations, you are meditating.

What do you think of when you think about meditation? Maybe you picture a monk, silently focusing for hours on end. Maybe you imagine someone sitting cross-legged and making "ohm" sounds. Maybe you think of someone trying their hardest to not think at all. These are all misconceptions about meditation that we have. In reality, meditation is mindfulness. It is relaxing and focusing, noticing everything around you physically and mentally. If you sit and close your eyes and try to notice every single thought you have, conscious and subconscious, you're meditating.

Why do so many people meditate? The real benefit of meditation, whether used in a spiritual or secular context, is to help you develop mindfulness. When you dedicate time in your day to focus on your mind, you slowly learn more and more about how you think. As you do so, you notice thought patterns you have, emotions you feel, and worries that affect you. Once you notice these things, you can begin to question them. Someone who meditates regularly has a much easier time figuring out why they feel stressed than someone who doesn't.

Self-awareness is an incredibly important piece for your mindfulness journey. You've probably been practicing self-awareness already, such as when you identify your negative thoughts and categorize them. When you are trying to improve your mindset to set yourself up for success, it is important to acknowledge that mindfulness is a necessary skill for you to develop. Mindfulness, which is the process of noticing your thoughts, is the most important facet of self-awareness. Meditation is the active pursuit of mindfulness. Things such as meditation can help you develop your mindfulness, and therefore bring you closer to your goal of establishing a positive mindset.

By now, you should have started having more positive thoughts courtesy of the self-appreciation technique that you are practicing. However, since your mind has been far too accustomed to negative thinking for a long time, it is possible that you are still likely to be prone to negative thoughts at times and this may greatly affect you.

Many people begin a new job or activity with a positive mindset, but somewhere along the way, their negative thinking patterns come back. A lot of things, such as stress or criticism, may disrupt your positive mindset. This is why it is important to practice mindfulness. Having this kind of awareness will help you eradicate all sorts of negative thoughts and get back on track.

Mindfulness refers to being aware of all that is happening around you. It makes you conscious of every thought that you have, so you can realize it and get rid of the ones that are not helping you. When you aren't mindful, you aren't able to recognize a negative thought right away. This gives negative ideas the opportunity to embed in your mind. Eventually, its roots begin to grow bigger. They will become more difficult to get rid of. Also, you will become more vulnerable to negativity. If you don't want that to happen to you, especially since you are making efforts towards improvement, you need to learn the art of mindfulness. Being mindful takes a lot of practice at first. Once you become completely familiar with it, it will happen naturally.

Slow Breathing and Affirmation

Meditation is a fantastic way to develop your mindfulness skills. However, it can be uncomfortable to start meditating out of the blue, especially with no prior knowledge. Sitting quietly and still with our thoughts for an extended period of time is not a normal part of life. Many who first start meditating experience discomfort. Sometimes, this discomfort stems from confronting thoughts you aren't used to, but most of the time, it's because you feel bored, stiff, and awkward. Because it's probably new, you should start as simple as possible. You can start with your breath. At random times during your day, such as lulls during work or after lunch, try to notice your breathing. You don't have to do anything special, simply notice your breath. Feel your lungs expanding and your chest rising and falling. After about a week, you'll be ready to start actually meditating. You'll still be practicing a very basic form of meditation, but the more you practice, the more comfortable it will be.

The basic technique to become mindful starts with your breathing. Begin by practicing slow breathing with positive affirmation. Start by inhaling and exhaling deeply or slowly. Put your mind at ease and pay attention to each breath. Remember that mindfulness largely relies on your breathing. You need to breathe in naturally, and with each breath you take, say 'I am mindful of myself.' This makes you focus on yourself and the things that are happening around you. Practice this for about five full minutes and carry out this exercise several times during the day.

When you breathe, you should count the number of seconds that you inhale and exhale. You can start with seven seconds in, eleven seconds out. This method gives your body plenty of oxygen and air to circulate your blood correctly. Since you are exhaling more than you are inhaling, you are also expelling extra carbon dioxide, which will help your circulation even more. Exhaling more than you inhale also gives you a sense of letting go, of freeing yourself, and it makes relaxation and stress-relief that much easier. Try to do this for at least five minutes. Seven seconds in, eleven seconds out. As you breathe, close your eyes and think about the numbers you are counting to. If other thoughts come to your mind, don't worry. Try to ignore them, but if you have trouble, and can't interrupt them with your counting, that's ok. You're learning how to meditate, and it won't come easily the first few times.

When you do this, you're meditating. I bet you never thought it was that easy. It really is. As you get better at it, you'll be adding more complexities to your meditations. But in the beginning, all you need to do is breathe and count. Mindfulness is a complex skill that takes a lot of practice to develop, so if you feel like this is starting slow, that's because it is. But as you practice more and more, you will begin to find it easier and easier to slip into a state of thought and breath.

Eventually, you'll get so used to counting your breaths that you'll start thinking about other things. Your affirmations, beginning with "I am mindful of myself," will help you center your thoughts on the task at hand. As you meditate, your goal should be to steady your breathing and your thoughts. Affirmations are a way for you to recenter the ideas flowing in your mind. Other affirmations include "I am capable," "I am calm," and "I am filled with purpose." Each of these phrases gives you something to focus on as you breathe, and they let you practice telling yourself positive things.

Concentration

The next step in developing your meditation skills is to learn how to concentrate. Concentration and focus are skills that many people have a shallow grasp of, but don't think to develop fully. Just like practicing a sport or instrument, if you put in time and effort into improving, your dedication will pay off. It is possible to improve your concentration skills. At first, you'll have very tangible thoughts to concentrate on. Counting your breaths and thinking affirmations will take focus to maintain for several minutes. But as you practice, it will get easier to do these things out of habit rather than with focus. So, eventually, you'll once again find your mind wandering. What do you do when that happens? Well, if you work on boosting your concentration skills, you'll be able to snap your focus back on the thoughts you want to think.

Make sure that you focus on nothing else but your breathing to become completely mindful of yourself. It will help if you start this activity in a quiet place. Let your mind become fully aware of exercise and filter any random thoughts and distractions. Your thoughts may wander at some points, but that's normal especially if you are new to this. Know that you can overcome any obstacle with enough time and effort. If you become interrupted, try and bring your focus again to your breathing. Practice this consistently to develop a more focused mind in any situation.

By using this practice regularly, you will train your brain to be more mindful of your surroundings. When you do this, try to notice things from all five of your senses. What can you feel? The chair you are sitting on, the clothes you are wearing, the breeze from the air conditioner. What can you hear? What can you taste? What can you smell? If your eyes are open, what can you see? Ask yourself these questions and try your hardest to only focus on the answers. As you do so, you will be getting your mind used to thinking only the most basic thoughts. You will eventually get used to these basic thoughts, so when you try to meditate, you won't get distracted by the repetitive affirmations you are giving yourself.

We live in an entertained world. Phones and computers and other devices are available at all times of the day to keep us entertained. It's rare to be bored; there is simply too much to look at. After a while, your mind gets used to this. It gets harder and harder to have banal, basic thoughts for long periods of time. Just like training for a marathon, if you are constantly having your mind run around, then when it comes time to slow down, what used to feel normal now feels incredibly boring. When you practice having these slow, meticulous thoughts, you are retraining your mind to be comfortable with that boredom. The more you practice, the easier it will become to focus and concentrate on the things around you.

As you practice, you will reach a stage of concentration in which it is easy to let thoughts pass through your mind, completely untouched, like cars driving down a highway. You'll be able to let your thoughts drift without actually thinking about them. In this state, you'd have complete control over what you're actively thinking about, even if your subconscious wants you to think about other things. This is the stage of meditation that you are working towards. Practice developing both your mindfulness, your breathing, and your concentration, until you can sit down and stop your thoughts altogether. Then, you can set aside a few minutes each day, maybe fifteen or twenty minutes, and you can meditate. Daily meditation will act as a chance to reset your mind.

Use Daily Tasks to Become Mindful

As you practice breathing and concentration techniques, you will eventually be able to become mindful even while walking and doing various chores. Being mindful even when involved in an activity seems like it requires more effort. After all, your mind handles a lot - from finishing tasks to running errands to interacting with different people. So, how can you achieve mindfulness in a busy, stressful environment? If you practice breathing exercises every day, then this should not be too much work for you. Just like focused breathing, learn how to be simply more aware of your actions. Be completely in the moment and take in the experience. What do you see around you? How does it make you feel? Pay attention to the little things that you commonly overlook. You can also use smartphone apps to help you incorporate mindfulness techniques in your daily schedule. Doing other activities that promote mindfulness, such as walking meditation, will also be beneficial.

Your mindfulness will extend to your daily tasks and activities. You can use this to your advantage. As your mindfulness improves, you can start practicing it even when you aren't meditating. When I first started developing mindfulness, I was meditating twice per day. Once in the morning and once at night. But, I noticed something strange. When I was at work, or driving, or at lunch, I would notice things that I never had before. Billboards on the road started to stand out. Posters in our break room that I had only glanced at now caught my attention. It was easier to recognize my own thoughts, whether they were positive, negative, or neutral. I could also recognize my emotions much easier. I could tell that I was feeling a specific emotion, and it was easier to pinpoint exactly what emotion it was. Even if I couldn't tell exactly what caused my thoughts, I could tell whether they were harmful to my mindset or not. Even my close friends and family noticed that I was more perceptive than normal. Meditating regularly has taught me how to notice my surroundings actively.

We all notice our surroundings passively. You see posters and advertisements and other things around you, but you rarely ever register them consciously. There are only so many things that our minds can actively think about. Normally, your brain simply files these peripheral things away, registering them but not alerting you to their presence. By meditating, you are practicing noticing things you don't usually pay attention to. Therefore, as you get better at meditating, you'll also gain better perception.

You should practice using the perception you have to apply mindfulness in your daily life. For example, you can apply it in meetings to help you read the emotions of the room with more ease. You can use it when talking to your boss to help you read between the lines of his instructions. A mindful driver is much better at reading traffic situations and avoiding accidents before they even happen. Your mindfulness will also help you react to the situations you are in. With mindfulness, you will be able to understand the emotions that drive your thoughts and actions. It will be easier to judge your immediate reaction to a situation you are in, and then decide on a course of action after brief reflection. Where before all your reactions were spur of the moment, mindfulness lets you take a step back and make a decision in a split second.

Once you learn how to be in the moment and mindful of everything around you, it becomes easier to identify harmful thoughts. You will gain the ability to easily notice whenever you are engaging in a negative thought process like mind reading, catastrophizing and such. This gives you the chance to take the necessary steps to stop negativity before it gets to you. For example, if you find yourself falling into over-generalizing, then you can stop yourself. Ask yourself why you are making these assumptions, how they make you feel, and what you are really worried about. Then, you can change your language so that you are thinking positive thoughts about the situation. If you can't think positive, you can at least think realistically and stop your negative thoughts in their tracks. The mindfulness you'll gain from meditation will make this process much easier. You'll have the answers to all the aforementioned questions much faster than before.

So far, you have learned how developing a positive mindset will help you. You know how to harness your subconscious, how to turn your negative thoughts into positive ones, and how to appreciate yourself. You have learned how to make yourself mindful of your thoughts, emotions, and external influences. The next two steps you will take in your journey to improve your mindset are to learn how to be a true optimist, and how to use science-backed techniques to stay as positive as possible.

Chapter 6: Finding the Good in Every Bad Situation

Many people hate the rain. It makes driving harder. It makes walking down the street a terrible chore. Rain floods roads, making huge puddles that drench any unfortunate pedestrians. Rain points out flaws. It gathers in poorly made ditches, it rests stagnant in puddles in uneven backyards. It points out holes in roofs and foundations. Leaky windows and doors are a disaster if they aren't caught early. Rain makes everything dark—the grey and black clouds that cover the sky cast the whole world into shade and gloom. If you like to exercise outdoors, you can't when it's raining. If you work outdoors, good luck getting what you need done while soaking wet. Any parent who's had to pull their kids out of the pool during rain knows how much they hate it, too. By most counts, rain only puts a damper on the day.

But for some, rain is a wonderful thing. For some people, rain is a sign of hope, growth, and change. Rain helps plants grow. Rain waters vegetation and soil, making all the land around you greener. The flooded roads means the local lake is full; there's no drought for now. It means you can save on your water bill and skip watering your lawn. Your backyard looks so much nicer when the grass is green and soft, instead of brown and dry. For some, even the sound of rain is a good thing. The soothing, rhythmic tapping of raindrops on a roof is comforting white noise that makes any room cozy. The smell of rain is relaxing and earthy, and it gives the outdoors a unique perfume.

For some, rain is a terrible inconvenience. For others, it's the highlight of their week. The only difference is in perspective. The objective truth remains the same: it is raining. But, depending on your mindset, you can react happily or glumly. How do you get yourself to react happily every time it rains? It all depends on your mindset.

The fifth and second to the last step to having a positive frame of mind is by enhancing your perspective to find the good in even the worst case scenarios.

Experiencing bad situations is a normal part of life, and it is vital that we learn how to handle them well.

Many times, people tend to look at situations in black or white. It's either good or bad. If you think of things this way, your actions become restricted and your options become limited. You begin to doubt yourself. If you don't learn how to find the good even in the bad situations, then you inevitably allow bad situations to remain as such.

Let's say your proposal at work didn't yield favourable results. You may think that you're a failure, and that you should just stop trying. However, if you take time to assess the situation, you will find that something good can come out of it. Instead of sulking over the negative outcome, think of it as a chance to do things differently. Maybe you should try an approach that you've never considered before. Maybe it's a chance for you to collaborate with your colleagues and see if it works.

When you can manage to find even a tiny ray of hope even in the dark times, you let yourself believe that there is still possibility for things to get better. This gives you the freedom of thinking clearly and liberating yourself from any doubts or limitations that bad experiences bring.

Here are a few tips that will help you figure out the good in worst situations:

• Find a quote that speaks to you. Print it and paste it in several places around your house and look at it numerous times during the day to become inspired. It will instil in you the hope that every bad situation is accompanied by something positive. You should try to memorize these quotes if possible. Some of the shorter ones are especially easy to commit to memory. Memorizing them will ensure that you can turn to them for comfort, even if you don't have them written anywhere. Of course, you should also write them in your journal and keep them somewhere accessible like your phone. Below are some examples of inspiring quotes to help you get started:

'Every bad situation will have something positive. Even a dead clock shows the correct time twice a day. Stay positive in life. God knows what's best for you....!'- Anonymous

'A problem is a chance for you to do your best.' - Duke Ellington

'The greater the difficulty, the more glory in surmounting it. Skillful pilots gain their reputation from storms and tempests.' - Epictetus

"Life is 10 percent what happens to you and 90 percent how you respond to it." -Charles Swindoll (Deschene, 2010)

"Fairy tales are more than true: not because they tell us that dragons exist, but because they tell us that dragons can be beaten."

— Neil Gaiman, Coraline (*Inspirational quotes*, 2019)

"Hope is the thing with feathers/ That perches in the soul/ And sings the tune without the words/ And never stops at all."

— Emily Dickinson (*Inspirational quotes*, 2019)

- There are also some longer quotes that I like to reflect on. I don't memorize these, instead I write them down once and then read them to myself once per day. I reflect on their meanings and on the context in which they were written. I always try to think about what they mean to me, how they make me feel, and how they can help me in my own life. I like to read one per day, a different one each day, so that my week always has these longer quotes to reflect on. Here are seven that I think you should read each day of the week.

"This life is what you make it. No matter what, you're going to mess up sometimes, it's a universal truth. But the good part is you get to decide how you're going to mess it up. Girls will be your friends - they'll act like it anyway. But just remember, some come, some go. The ones that stay with you through everything - they're your true best friends. Don't let go of them. Also remember, sisters make the best friends in the world. As for lovers, well, they'll come and go too. And baby, I hate to say it, most of them - actually pretty much all of them are going to break your heart, but you can't give up because if you give up, you'll never find your soulmate. You'll never find that half who makes you whole and that goes for everything. Just because you fail once, doesn't mean you're gonna fail at everything. Keep trying, hold on, and always, always, always believe in yourself, because if you don't, then who will, sweetie? So keep your head high, keep your chin up, and most importantly, keep smiling, because life's a beautiful thing and there's so much to smile about."

— Marilyn Monroe (*Inspirational quotes*, 2019)

"It is not the critic who counts; not the man who points out how the strong man stumbles, or where the doer of deeds could have done them better. The credit belongs to the man who is actually in the arena, whose face is marred by dust and sweat and blood; who strives valiantly; who errs, who comes short again and again, because there is no effort without error and shortcoming; but who does actually strive to do the deeds; who knows great enthusiasms, the great devotions; who spends himself in a worthy cause; who at the best knows in the end the triumph of high achievement, and who at the worst, if he fails, at least fails while daring greatly, so that his place shall never be with those cold and timid souls who neither know victory nor defeat."

— Theodore Roosevelt (*Inspirational quotes*, 2019)

"We're all seeking that special person who is right for us. But if you've been through enough relationships, you begin to suspect there's no right person, just different flavors of wrong. Why is this? Because you yourself are wrong in some way, and you seek out partners who are wrong in some complementary way. But it takes a lot of living to grow fully into your own wrongness. And it isn't until you finally run up against your deepest demons, your unsolvable problems—the ones that make you truly who you are—that we're ready to find a lifelong mate. Only then do you finally know what you're looking for. You're looking for the wrong person. But not just any wrong person: it's got to be the right wrong person—someone you lovingly gaze upon and think, "This is the problem I want to have. I will find that special person who is wrong for me in just the right way."

— Andrew Boyd, Daily Afflictions: The Agony of Being Connected to Everything in the Universe (*Inspirational quotes*, 2019)

"Pain is a pesky part of being human, I've learned it feels like a stab wound to the heart, something I wish we could all do without, in our lives here. Pain is a sudden hurt that can't be escaped. But then I have also learned that because of pain, I can feel the beauty, tenderness, and freedom of healing. Pain feels like a fast stab wound to the heart. But then healing feels like the wind against your face when you are spreading your wings and flying through the air! We may not have wings growing out of our backs, but healing is the closest thing that will give us that wind against our faces."

— C. JoyBell C. (*Inspirational quotes*, 2019)

"Dear God," she prayed, "let me be something every minute of every hour of my life. Let me be gay; let me be sad. Let me be cold; let me be warm. Let me be hungry...have too much to eat. Let me be ragged or well dressed. Let me be sincere - be deceitful. Let me be truthful; let me be a liar. Let me be honorable and let me sin. Only let me be something every blessed minute. And when I sleep, let me dream all the time so that not one little piece of living is ever lost."

— Betty Smith, A Tree Grows in Brooklyn (*Inspirational quotes*, 2019)

"We are going to die, and that makes us the lucky ones. Most people are never going to die because they are never going to be born. The potential people who could have been here in my place but who will in fact never see the light of day outnumber the sand grains of Arabia. Certainly those unborn ghosts include greater poets than Keats, scientists greater than Newton. We know this because the set of possible people allowed by our DNA so massively exceeds the set of actual people. In the teeth of these stupefying odds it is you and I, in our ordinariness, that are here.We privileged few, who won the lottery of birth against all odds, how dare we whine at our inevitable return to that prior state from which the vast majority have never stirred?"

— Richard Dawkins, Unweaving the Rainbow: Science, Delusion and the Appetite for Wonder (*Inspirational quotes*, 2019)

"What are you going to do with your life?" In one way or another it seemed that people had been asking her this forever; teachers, her parents, friends at three in the morning, but the question had never seemed this pressing and still she was no nearer an answer... "Live each day as if it's your last', that was the conventional advice, but really, who had the energy for that? What if it rained or you felt a bit glandy? It just wasn't practical. Better by far to be good and courageous and bold and to make difference. Not change the world exactly, but the bit around you. Cherish your friends, stay true to your principles, live passionately and fully and well. Experience new things. Love and be loved, if you ever get the chance."

— David Nicholls, One Day (*Inspirational quotes*, 2019)

• Whenever you experience a bad situation, you need to write it down in detail in your journal. Go through it in depth to find out any positive point that you have missed. You are bound to find something positive if you keep looking at the situation from different angles. Every situation in our lives has good, bad, and neutral aspects to them. By writing them down, you give yourself an opportunity that few people ever have access to. You can go back and dissect every decision you made. You can reflect on each and every point where you made a choice, or where a choice was made for you, and think of all the positives, negatives, and neutral things that resulted from those choices. For example, say your car breaks down on the side of the road. Obviously, this is a negative experience. But, the way you handle it can help shape how you feel about it. For example, if you react calmly, it will be easier for you to think, and therefore easier to find solutions to the issue at hand. When you look back at the situation, you can pinpoint exactly where you made good or bad decisions. Say you have never had a flat tire before, so when you get one you panic and can't remember how to fix it. Now, you have to call, if you have cell service, and get your car towed. A calm reaction would let you think through the steps for changing your tire. When you journal, you'll have the opportunity to remember that mistake, so that the second time you change your tire, you remember that you should stay calm. That's a positive outcome. It's learning. Even when you can't find anything positive about a specific situation, remind yourself that learning from your mistakes is one of the best ways for you to grow as a person. Journaling these bad situations help you learn lessons from them faster.

• Keep telling yourself, 'There's a way out' loudly and clearly. This affirmation will help your mind think clearly to find a way out of the situation you may be in. Remember that a calm mind is a decisive one. Constantly reminding yourself that you have a way out of a situation will help your subconscious register this fact. Then, with your subconscious calmed down, you can begin to calm your conscious thoughts. Calming your conscious thoughts is much easier when your subconscious is already subdued. If you try to do this the other way, trying to calm your conscious thoughts before your subconscious ones, then that underlying fear and anxiety will not go away. This is why the affirmation is so effective. With it, you can put all your focus into the affirmation, which lets you direct your conscious thoughts, putting them out of the way temporarily. Now, you can breathe and relax, so that your subconscious calms down. Then, you can stop the affirmation and address your conscious thoughts. You are now free to think of a way out of your situation. Other affirmations have a similar effect. You can try saying, "I can do this," or "This is temporary." Whatever affirmation you choose, make sure your affirmation focuses on a few key things. First, it should somehow remind you that the situation you are in will end. Second, it should remind you that you are able to make choices that affect the situation. Third, it should unite these two ideas without making you feel guilty for the situation you are in, especially if it is something out of your control. Repeat these affirmations to yourself while you are in a tough situation and you will find it much easier to get out.

• Channel your energy into creativity. You don't need to be artistic to try your hand at something new. Instead of keeping your negative feelings to yourself, use it to create something. The act of creating art has a powerful effect on the mind. It is calming, reassuring, and often helps to build confidence, even if you don't think your art is "good." Anyone can make art that is good, because the only qualification for "good" art is that it makes you happy. If singing along to music makes you happy, then belt those lyrics, no matter how out of tune your singing is. If you find joy in painting, then paint as much as you can, no matter how misshapen your trees are. The purpose of this art is not to make money or to end up in a museum. The purpose of this art is to make you happy. It should make you feel calm. It should make you feel reassured in your own abilities. Working with your hands is incredibly rewarding, and creating art often involves working with your hands. You'll be surprised how much confidence you gain when you let yourself enjoy the art you create. I like to paint, and so, when I'm feeling particularly stressed, I'll watch painting videos that help the viewer follow along. When the painting is finished, I hang it up in front of my workspace at home. Now, I have something pretty to look at when I'm working that I made. It's an instant confirmation that I am capable of creating nice things. I'm not a very good painter, but that doesn't matter. Making those paintings brings me joy. Looking at them reminds me of that joy. Hanging them up makes me feel accomplished. By channeling your energy into creativity, you can foster these feelings in yourself as well.

• Find inspiration from others. Chances are, there is someone who has also gone through something similar. Read some books or blogs and learn from other people's stories. You'll find bits of advice that you can use in battling your own problems. Everyone is unique, but most experiences are shared. If you're struggling with something, it's incredibly unlikely that your struggle is brand new. Online communities are excellent for bringing together people with shared experiences. You'd be surprised at just how diverse and specific these communities can be. If you can think of a profession, there's an online forum about it. If you have a specific question, you can research it and it's incredibly likely that you aren't the first person to ask. There are interviews, speeches, and talks that are very easy to access and have to do with specific struggles that many people face in life. The internet hosts a plethora of enriching content, you just have to look for it. Offline help is abundant as well. Books and magazines have been publishing self-help tips for decades. Newspapers often have advice columns that can help you as well. You can find more generalized advice in offline content. Since it costs money to print something offline, it usually needs to have a larger target audience than online content does. That can be a disadvantage, but it is also a good thing. For example, you can find generalized self-help content in hundreds of books. These books can help you overcome a large number of issues without addressing your specific needs. This book is a great example of books that offer advice in a more generalized way. Wherever you find it, you can rest assured that advice is just a click or page flip away.

• Recall your times of victory. When was the last time you overcame something difficult? Remind yourself that you are capable of rising above any situation. This is why journaling is so important. If you are writing down events where you felt victorious, then you can read about them instead of trying to remember all the details. You should set aside time everyday to write about your losses and victories, and read about your previous days as well. The more you do this, the easier it will get. You'll also get progressively better at conveying your emotions, identifying types of situations, and remembering to write it down in the first place. Your times of victory are key to your personal development. When you remember them, you are also remembering the events that led up to and followed them, as well as all the key decisions you made along the way. This will let you remember how it feels to make good decisions, have your choices pay off, and how it felt to really, truly do something good for yourself. Reminding yourself of those feelings will make you relive them. Just like how thinking negative thoughts makes you feel bad, or how thinking about embarrassing situations makes you feel embarrassed, thinking about your past victories will make you feel victorious. Your mindset will improve when you remind yourself of how it feels to be victorious.

• Think about how this situation will help you. Tough times may give you doubt, problems and other unpleasant things. However, it can also help you develop qualities that will be useful in the future. These difficult battles can prepare you and make you more resilient to the challenges the future may bring. When I think about hardships, I like to think of a metaphor from my childhood. A good gardener does not leave all his plants to grow on their own. If they were allowed to grow freely, they would quickly become overgrown, competing with each other and suffering for it. A good gardener will trim plants, pull weeds, and prevent the plants from overstepping each other. Now, the plants have room to grow. If a rosebush goes untrimmed, it will grow leaves and the flowers will suffer. If a gardener trims the leaves and thorns of the rosebush, the bush will be able to use its resources on its flowers, and the roses will be much more beautiful. Hardships happen to all of us. They are as normal as breathing. But your reaction to them can determine whether they are worth anything. If you treat tough times as a learning opportunity, as space to grow, you will reap benefits from those times. If you treat tough times as pure punishment, you won't learn anything. You'll end up wallowing in your negative emotions without any room to grow. Hardship without an optimistic attitude is just like the untrimmed rosebush. Too many resources spent on negative things. As often as you can, try to trim your rosebush, so that all you can grow are beautiful flowers.

• Remind yourself of the saying, "This too shall pass." This old phrase, a story from childhood, is still relevant now. It's a reminder that your feelings and situations are temporary, and that the things which afflict you are not going to affect you forever. "This too shall pass" is an incredibly powerful phrase and you should be using it much more than you probably are. When you are feeling down, it can remind you that you won't always feel bad. And when you're happy, it reminds you to cherish those good moments while you can. Someone with a positive mindset knows that negative situations are not eternal and that no mistake is completely permanent. People with positive mindsets also know that expecting happiness 24/7 is not a good thing. If you expect yourself to be happy constantly, then when you feel down or even just neutral, you will feel like you have failed in some way. You'll blame yourself for something that is completely natural. Imagine getting upset with yourself every time it rained. You don't have any control over the clouds, so why would you waste your energy on blaming yourself? You experience the same waste of energy every time you expect yourself to be happy when you aren't. It's not failing to feel upset or neutral—it's human. Remind yourself, as much as you can, that your emotions are temporary. Your state of being is completely separate. You can have a positive, optimistic mindset on life and feel sad. Sadness is your emotion, positivity is your state of being. In this book and throughout your life, you should be striving to achieve a state of positivity, not a feeling of happiness.

• When you rely on others, you grow closer to them. As you move through life, you will no doubt experience many, many periods of strife. When you do, remember that as you reach out to loved ones and friends for help, you will strengthen those friendships. Reaching out to people shows them that you trust them. It also shows that you value their ideas, beliefs, and experiences enough to ask them for help in your own life. This is a show of friendship beyond anything words can express. We show our love for people with our actions. While words do help, actions are much more potent. When you ask someone for support in a tough situation, you are taking action to show how much you care about them. From then on, no matter how the situation ends up resolving, you can be sure that you will be closer to that person than you were before. As humans, we crave social interaction like it's food. You can use the idea of growing closer to a friend to motivate you to move through a difficult situation. If you reach out to that friend, coworker, or family member, you will be closer to them when all is said and done. Remind yourself of this when you are in the midst of a tough trial. It can be incredibly encouraging to know that no matter how the situation ends, whether good or bad, you will have a better friend at your side. Over time, this effect will only amplify. Better yet, if your issue is feelings of loneliness, deepening a friendship will probably solve your problem. In a tough situation, know that you aren't the only one who will grow from it.

● One thing people can do to improve their mood in a bad situation is to listen to someone close to them talk about something they love. Whenever you are feeling down, try to cherish the things other people love. You can distract yourself from a difficult situation by focusing on the people around you. If you have a friend or family member who is enthusiastic about something, let them teach you about it. Even if you aren't particularly interested in specifics, you'll get to be around someone who is passionate. You can be around someone who is showing true care for a thing they love. Being around that kind of person will remind you of all the things that you cherish in life. Maybe you aren't a fan of the TV show your friend is gushing about, but their enthusiasm reminds you of a show that you love and how watching it makes you happy. You might not care about the stock market at all, but when your spouse talks about it, the light in their eyes reminds you of why you love your own job. By letting people share their interests with you, you will be reminded of your own. Now, when you are in a tough situation, especially when it involves negative emotions, you can remind yourself of those passionate conversations. When you remind yourself of them, you will feel some of the excitement that your friend felt. You can then use that excitement to bolster your own mood.

• Always try to remind yourself that you can't control everything. There are always situations in life that you cannot control. There are always times when something bad happens to you for no reason other than chance. It is so easy to feel discouraged when this happens. You are learning to be in tune with your mental state, to control your thoughts and emotions, and to try to always look on the bright side of things. When an event in your life is completely outside of your control, it can feel like all your progress has been erased. To combat this, I want you to write down in your journal the things about the situation that you can and can't control. Which aspects of this issue are in your hands and which are in the hands of fate? A good way to figure this out is to ask yourself what changes when you are removed from the equation. Say you just got rear-ended at a stop sign. You're bound to be pretty upset, that's normal. Which part of the situation can you control? Could you have prevented the car from hitting you? Well, if you weren't there, they probably would have either hit the car in front of you, or driven into oncoming traffic. So, they would have been in an accident either way. The car hitting you is out of your control. Try your hardest to not be upset about the things you can't control. It does you no good to worry about them. What do your negative emotions change about the circumstances? Nothing. All it does is make you more stressed and upset. Take the energy you have towards the uncontrollable things and direct it to controllable ones. You can't control the car that hit you, but you can control how you react. Focus on reminding yourself that some things simply can't be changed, and focus on changing only what you have the power to change.

• Do one nice thing every day. This rule seems simple on the surface, but in reality it is an extraordinarily powerful tool at your disposal. People with positive mindsets see the strangers around them as potential friends, not as enemies or inconveniences. Treat those around you as you would your friends, and do something nice for them every chance you get. This is a big habit to form, especially if you are used to putting your head down and minding your own business. So to start, try to always do one nice thing per day. Write down the nice things you do for people in your journal, as well as how they make you feel. You might not feel much of anything if the action is simple enough, but that's not the point. Hold the door for someone, pay for the person behind you in line at the drive-thru, give a coworker a compliment. It doesn't matter how small the action is. You never know how much a simple act can affect someone, so don't judge your actions on size. Instead, focus on the number of these little kindnesses you do per day. Start with one every day. Once it is second nature to at least do one, you can start making a conscious effort to do more. As you add in numbers to your generous acts, it will get easier and easier to do them without even thinking. When you reach this state, your subconscious, not your conscious, will be looking for nice things to do for others. Then, you will see those around you as potential friends. It is much easier to navigate the world with this perspective. You will see kindness in the hearts of every stranger you meet. This will make your everyday routine much more optimistic.

• No matter how busy you are, always let yourself take a day off. If you're particularly stressed, you might not be giving yourself true days off. Yes, your 9 to 5 is giving you Saturday and Sunday off, but what are you doing on those days? Chores? Errands? That's not a day off, that's housework. If your job is very stressful, you may be thinking about work on your weekend even if you aren't doing other types of work. Stress is mental work. If you're stressing about your job on the weekend, you aren't taking a day off. Time off is incredibly valuable. It lets you reset your mind, relax your subconscious, and refreshes your attitude towards the work you do. If you aren't giving yourself at least one day off per week, then you are hurting your mental health and your mindset. How can you expect yourself to have a positive mindset when you are always thinking about your job? Your brain needs breaks just as much as your body does. Plan a day per week, Saturday or Sunday, or if your work schedule is more unique, then during the normal work week. Whatever day it is, make sure it is consistent week after week, so that you establish a routine. On that day, don't do any work. Don't do chores, don't do errands, don't even think about working. Give yourself a relaxing task that you like doing, such as a craft or physical activity, and focus on that throughout your day. It doesn't have to take up your whole day, it just needs to be enough to distract you from work. Use the day to relax and reset your mind. You'll very likely find that you are more productive, more confident, and maybe even more creative on the day after your day off.

• Always remember that progress is not a straight line. This has been said several times in this book, but it's in this list, too. That's because it is one of the most important lessons in self-improvement. Throughout your journey, you will struggle. It will be hard to do all the practices sometimes. It will be hard to replace negative words, to remember to journal, to meditate. That does not mean you are going backwards. It doesn't mean you have failed. When you experience setbacks like these, tell yourself that it is simply a curve on the path of progress. When I think of this phrase, I like to think about the Grand Canyon. It is one of the most beautiful landmarks in the world. A huge carving in the earth, hundreds of feet deep, with a roaring river flowing through it. That river, the Colorado River, made the canyon it now flows through. The Grand Canyon was carved over a period of thousands of years, one grain of sand at a time, until the final product was formed. It is still being carved today, and in another thousand years, it will look completely different than it does now. And this deep canyon, carved by nothing but flowing water, has curves. It has twists and turns, valleys, and hills. It is uneven and deeper in some places than others. In some spots the river flows gently, while in others the white water rapids are incredibly dangerous to traverse. The river that made the Grand Canyon is no less important because of these twists and turns or the slow and fast spots. It's journey is not a straight line. And that is what makes it beautiful.

• Whenever you feel you are truly at a loss, reach out to others. This tip is very hard for some people to act upon. For many, asking for help is uncomfortable. No one wants to burden their friends and family with their troubles. To overcome this hesitation, imagine how you would feel if a friend reached out to you. When your friends come to you for help, do you feel burdened? Overwhelmed? Uncomfortable? Most of the time, the answer is no. Unless your friends are being truly overbearing and are overstepping a boundary, when they ask for help, you are more than willing to give it to them. You aren't a licensed therapist, but you're ready to be a hand to hold, a shoulder to cry on, a listening ear. If you are willing to support your friends and family, then they are also willing to support you. You should make an effort to always think of them as a system of support that you can reach out to whenever you are feeling down. If you have a problem you can't fix, and you've exhausted all your options, ask someone close to you for advice. Even if they can't think of a way to fix your problem, the act of explaining it to them can be enough to help you think of a brand new solution. If your friends and family truly care about you, they won't want to see you suffer. They will find joy in helping you through hardship and strife. Reach out to them. Use your support system. It is a truly beneficial tool for anyone struggling to improve their mindset.

Practice these simple tips and in due time, you will find it easier to see a positive opportunity in every bad situation. That is the true mark of a positive mindset. Not being constantly happy, not always having good things happen to you. It's impossible to make the right choices every single time you have the option to choose. A true positive mindset is when you can look at a situation and figure out how to be optimistic about it. To take this one step further, a positive mindset is knowing in situations where you can't possibly see a positive opportunity that it does not mean the world is coming to an end. There are situations we come across that are just plain bad. Death is a particularly hurtful example of this. It can be impossible to see a positive when it comes to death. If you can't find one, don't blame yourself. With a true positive mindset, you'll be able to recognize that even though there are no positive outcomes of this situation, this is not the only situation you will ever be in. A true positive mindset involves unconditional understanding of yourself. These tips are designed to help you achieve that mindset. They will help you put events into perspective. They will help you navigate the world even when you can't see the light at the end of the tunnel. When you finally develop your positive mindset, you will know at all times that if you keep walking, you'll find the light.

Chapter 7: Practicing NLP Techniques for Developing a Positive Mindset

You wake up to your alarm blaring, but as you go to turn it off, you realize that it's twenty minutes late. You must have hit snooze while half asleep. You rush out of bed, short on time due to your accidental sleeping in. You don't have time to do your morning routine, so you can't meditate or write in your journal. All you can do is get ready, get dressed, and start driving to work. You're leaving the house later than normal, so now the traffic is much worse than you're used to. It takes an extra fifteen minutes to drive to work. You're extra late now. You finally get to work, upset, anxious, and disoriented. Your manager is upset with you too, and so is the coworker who was doing your work for the last half an hour. As you start working, the stress of the morning doesn't leave you. You make mistake after mistake as you rush through the day. You don't have the energy to think about any of your mindfulness practices that you've been working on. You even forget to check on your emotions. All of your thoughts are negative, so what are you supposed to do—not think? You're tired and stressed and your whole desk is as disorganized as your thoughts. All through the day it's like this. Now, your mood is bitter. You see sneers on every face in the office, and you worry your boss is talking about you to his boss. You know he's mad and he's probably going to fire you soon. You're sure he was just waiting for a chance. You've handed him one on a silver platter. At the end of the day, you can't wait to get home and just relax after this terrible disaster. Of course, it's not that easy. There's massive traffic on your commute home, too, and there's an accident or two, because the universe knows you're ready to get home so it wants you to spend some quality time sitting on tarmac in your car parked on the highway for half an hour. Finally, you get home. You're even more upset now, humiliated by your work day and angry from your commute. You decide to order food to be delivered to spare yourself from the chore of cooking. But the order is so much more expensive with all the fees and it takes an hour to get to you. Now, you're hungry and angry and frustrated and ashamed. You go to bed with a knot of rage in your stomach. What a terrible day.

With all the progress you've made and all the techniques you've learned in the last few chapters, you're probably feeling really good about your mindset. That's wonderful! But remember, progress isn't a straight line. If you feel yourself slipping at times, falling back into negative thought patterns, forgetting to meditate regularly, or are just plain having a bad day, that's perfectly normal. What should you do in those situations? Mope? Give up on the day? Stop trying to improve your mindset? Resign yourself to a lack of success and progress? Of course not. Instead, you can use some psychological tricks to jumpstart your mental health. These tricks will help you put your experiences into perspective and trick your brain into feeling positive emotions. That way, when you're having bad days or periods of slow to no progress, you can use these techniques to improve your mood and start back on your path to a positive mindset.

If you have been committed to your goal and have been implementing all the techniques discussed previously in the book, then you are doing an amazing job. You just have one more chapter to go for you to learn how to unlock the power of positive thinking. To bring you closer to your goal, this chapter will teach you a couple of fantastic NLP techniques for developing and boosting a positive mindset.

First, what is NLP? NLP or neuro-linguistic programming is a term invented by Dr. Richard Bandler in the 1970s. He defined the term as "a system of alternative therapy based on this which seeks to educate people in self-awareness and effective communication, and to change their patterns of mental and emotional behaviour." This means that neuro-linguistic programming looks at mental health as a personal journey. It focuses on helping the patient learn more about themselves so that they can shift their thought patterns on their own. If you could change your own mental and emotional behavior, you probably would in a heartbeat. So, NLP seeks to teach you how to do just that.

Through NLP, patients are encouraged to seek change from within. Therapists who practice NLP try to bring their patients to recognize the sources for change within themselves. Meditation falls under the umbrella of NLP techniques. In helping you improve your self-awareness, meditation leads you to the solutions to many common issues. With NLP, you'll learn to harness your own thoughts to do more than just control your emotions. NLP can be used to help patients overcome phobias or traumatic events. It's using your own mental fortitude to rewire your thinking.

In other words, NLP is a brilliant personal development, psychotherapy and communication approach that benefits you in a number of ways. It is designed to help you develop positive thinking. Without going into more details of NLP techniques, here are two amazing NLP techniques that will be truly beneficial in assisting you to achieve a positive mindset.

Self-Anchoring

Self-anchoring is a technique that helps you experience a positive emotion upon saying or doing something that you have anchored that response with. Start by identifying a state you are interested in experiencing; for instance, self-confidence. Next, do something that makes you feel confident. For instance, it could be speaking a positive affirmation. Once, you are in that state, start imagining a big smoke circle. Step inside that circle and slowly feel positive energy engulfing you. Then, step out of that circle and think of anything irrelevant to that emotion. Think of unrelated ideas and other distractions. And then, step in the circle after five minutes and observe how you feel. If you start feeling confident and happy, then you are starting to learn the technique of self-anchoring. If not, then you should continue to practice stepping into and out of the circle until you anchor it in your mind. Don't worry if it doesn't work for you right away. Keep practicing this technique and you will eventually realize its effects.

The images you imagine don't necessarily have to be exactly these. The most important thing is that you are taking a vivid mental image, a specific emotion or feeling, and tying them together with a movement. For example, I had a friend for whom the circle with smoke just wasn't working, so she made her own image and movement. She would imagine herself standing on the edge of a lake. She grew up near one so this image was comforting for her. Then, she would make herself feel her target emotion, whatever she chose it to be. Next she would envision herself walking into the water, one step at a time, slowly going deeper into cold water until she was completely submerged. At this point in the mental exercise, she would actually hold her breath, and then she would imagine herself stepping out of the water, step by step, until she emerged soaking wet on the shore. When she did this, she would actually walk and take each step in real life just as she did in her imagination. It worked better for her because she was able to incorporate several senses that she was intimately familiar with. She could practically smell the lake's waters. She could feel the cold water as she stepped into it. She knew exactly what it felt like to walk into the lake, and she could imagine it perfectly. Holding her breath and walking created a strong association between the mental image and the movements. She also told me that the first few times she did this exercise, she didn't use her target emotion. She just practiced tying the movement and the mental image together. Once she was comfortable with the bond between those two, she added the target emotion. If you are struggling to anchor yourself, try to approach this practice like my friend did. You should see rapid results.

Self-anchoring will help you if you are having trouble replacing negative thoughts and emotions in your day-to-day life. Instead of struggling to identify and replace the negative words, you can use your anchor to bring yourself back to a positive attitude. This works by training yourself to associate that mood with a physical movement. This movement, the anchor, lets you return to that mood just by imagining it. Just like the muscle memory you developed for your subconscious, this is muscle memory for your emotions. When you do an action, you feel a certain emotion.

Self-anchoring is a type of psychological process called conditioning. You can condition your brain to think a certain thing when you are given a specific trigger. Conditioning was revolutionized by a famous psychologist, Pavalov. He trained dogs to be conditioned to expect food when they heard a bell. By ringing a bell every time he fed them, the dogs learned that the bell meant food was on the way. Then, all Pavalov had to do was ring the bell, and the dogs would start salivating as though they were ready to eat. If you have dogs, you've probably trained them in a similar way, even accidentally. When I put my shoes on in the morning, my dogs get excited, because they know that I'm about to take them on a walk. For you, stepping into the imaginary circle is the bell and feeling confident is the food. You can condition yourself to feel that emotion without meeting the normal requirements for feeling it.

The process of tying these two together will take a while. Self-anchoring requires patience to be done right. You may feel awkward doing it at first, especially if it's hard for you to form mental images. But with enough repetition, you will train yourself to anchor the movement to the emotion. If you've been following along with the practices in this book so far, then you have probably already done a form of self-anchoring. When you sit down to meditate, how does it make you feel? Do you feel relaxed as you prepare, without actually meditating? If you do, then congratulations, you've already anchored yourself with your meditation. Just the act of sitting down and then calming down means that your brain associates sitting with being calm. Now, whenever you sit in your meditation spot, your brain associates it with relaxation, and the effects begin immediately.

This associative effect can work for other methods. You should try the above practice as much as you can, but you can also anchor yourself to actions such as sitting or stretching. Things like listening to specific music or watching a specific show can also help you sink into your desired emotion. You probably already have something like this in your life and just haven't realized it. NLP is based on your inherent capability to heal yourself, so if you've been experimenting with self-help methods for your negative moods, it's easy to stumble across an NLP technique. The more you train your mind to react to an outside stimulus, the stronger that bond will become. Practice makes perfect. You should be repeating this practice at least once per day until you can feel the tangible change in your mood when you do it. Then, continue doing it at least once a day, but at times when you need to feel your target emotion. Giving yourself self-confidence right before running a presentation is an almost magical tool at your disposal, and all you need to do to get it is a little practice.

Content Reframing

For content reframing, I like to ask people a very simple question. Can you remember an embarrassing moment that embarrassed someone else? Not one of your embarrassments, someone else's? You probably can't. If you can, you have to dig around in your memory to think of an event that could have been embarrassing for a friend. But for the most part, you can't even think of something that someone *should* have been embarrassed about, much less something that actually embarrassed them. Why is that? We tend to amplify our own emotions in other people's minds. This is a form of mind reading. Mind reading, over-generalizing, and catastrophizing are all negative thought patterns that are greatly mitigated by content reframing.

Take any bad episode that has happened to you and ponder over your feelings associated with it. For instance, a bad interview. What feeling does it bring? It may be self-doubt, disappointment or shame. Now imagine yourself ten years from now and think how you would perceive that episode. Would you still feel embarrassed over it? It is probable that it won't seem as intimidating as it was when you first experienced it. Perhaps you would feel confident of yourself if anything similar happened again. This is what content reframing does. It reshapes a bad situation into a positive one, so that it wouldn't have the same negative effect on you again. Apply this tactic to different situations in your life to transform bad experiences into positive and uplifting ones.

You can't remember those embarrassing moments because it was only embarrassing for your friend. So now, you can recognize that all those embarrassing moments that you still think about, like that one time in middle school that keeps you up at night for some reason, are not thought about or remembered by anyone but you. Once you recognize this, you are reframing the content of whatever is worrying you, hence the name of this method. It works wonders for other emotions as well. For example, you can take a moment where you made a mistake you regret and think about what you learned from it. Maybe you got into a fender bender in traffic, and now you know to pay extra attention even when you're driving slow. You can reframe the content of a bad memory by thinking about where you went in life and the different path you've gone down because of it.

You can also use time to reframe the content of your mood or memory. It's incredibly frustrating to be stuck in traffic, but by tomorrow you probably won't even care. When you find yourself experiencing an emotion, ask yourself how long you think it will last. Just a few hours? A day? A week? In the moment, our emotions seem like they will last forever, especially if they're extreme. But, as you know from developing your self-awareness, emotions come and go, and they don't last for as long as they seem. Pay attention to how long you experience your more potent emotions. Try to write down how long they last, so that in the future, when you experience them again, you can look back and reflect on how temporary they are.

For memories, you can use content reframing to remind yourself that memories fade in potency over time. An embarrassing memory will become less embarrassing as time goes on, and you'll probably forget it after a while. A sad memory will become less sad as you adjust and reflect. Happy memories also are subject to this. Try to notice when you are in a situation that will leave happy memories. Take pictures, journal about the details, and go back and remember when you are feeling down. Just like you can make a negative emotion feel like it lasted minutes, you can make a positive one feel like it lasts weeks. Our memories ebb and flow with the passage of time, and you, with your excellent control over your mindset, can harness this to benefit your thoughts. All it takes is practice.

It's important to remember when you're content reframing that just because an emotion is temporary, that doesn't mean that it is invalid. When you feel frustrated in traffic, or embarrassed by saying the wrong thing, or upset at something that was said to you, it's ok to feel that emotion. The purpose of content reframing is to help you shift your perspective so that the emotion doesn't seem never ending. Even though you're sad now, soon you won't be. Remind yourself frequently of how long each of your emotions tends to last. This practice requires a very high level of self-awareness that not everyone has. If you're struggling to figure out how to reframe the content of emotions and memories, that's completely normal. The more you practice, the easier it will become to shift your own perspective.

Practice these two techniques as much as possible and apply them in the situations that you face. It will promote and maintain positivity in your mind. Also, it will help you develop a forward-thinking perspective that focuses on the good side of things. Remember that this is an ongoing process. At some point, you may think that you've achieved the confidence that you want, but just keep going and don't stop. Remember one of the key teachings in this book—progress is not a straight line. In order to permanently change your mindset, you need to establish thinking habits that extend far beyond a few weeks of practice. My journey to a successful mindset has taken years to develop, and it's constantly growing and changing with time. The best thing you can do for yourself is be patient. Especially when it comes to these NLP techniques, the skills take a long time to develop into something useful. It takes even longer to make them a habit. Don't be discouraged if these processes don't work immediately. If your mindset slips into negativity every once and a while, that doesn't mean you've failed. It means you're human. You aren't going to reach a state of perfection as you embark on this journey. We are always learning and improving. Your goal should not be perfect mastery of NLP techniques; it should be to get a little better at them, day by day, week by week, year by year. Only with this mindset will you be able to find true success on your journey.

Conclusion

It is close to impossible to be successful unless you have a positive frame of mind. After all, achieving a goal starts with having the right mindset and breaking free from your limitations. So, if you are completely certain that you want to reach the pinnacle of success and accomplish all your goals and objectives, then you must exercise every single technique discussed in this guide. Getting started may be challenging or overwhelming, but once you learn how to transform your mind, you will gain something that can't be taken away from you.

Now, you should know exactly what it takes to establish a positive mindset. You know why you need a better mindset and that you have a world of possibilities waiting for you when you approach your life's journey with the right frame of mind. You also know that the underlying cause of your mindset change is your subconscious. You learned how your subconscious works, how to control it, and methods for influencing your subconscious to your advantage. You also learned how to think positive thoughts. You are now able to recognize different types of negative thoughts so that you can address them as they come up. You can also go a step further and swap negative words for positive ones in your speech and thoughts. Even more than that, you can turn your thoughts positive and you know how to practice praising yourself. Finally, you can go one more step and add "yet" to your thoughts when you can't seem to otherwise turn them around. You should now be a self-care and self-appreciation master. You know all about what it means to appreciate yourself and how to do so in a sustainable, unprideful way. You are on your way to becoming completely in tune with your thoughts, and through meditation, you will develop that more and more. Your optimism is through the charts, and you can repeat positive reminders to yourself whenever you need them. Lastly, you've learned scientific techniques for improving your thoughts and mood that, with enough practice, will pull you out of just about any bad mood.

What is success? All throughout this book, your goal has been to develop a positive mindset and set yourself up for success. What does that mean? How does being positive translate to success in life? First, let's define success. The specifics change from person to person, and even from day to day. But in general, success is achieving a goal that you set out to accomplish. It is deciding to do a task and then completing it. There are varying degrees of success. You can succeed by the bare minimum, you can overachieve, or you can even go above and beyond in accomplishing what you set out to do. Whatever you choose to define success as, specifically, you are chasing it with every professional and casual goal you have. Once you achieve your goal successfully, what do you do? You probably set another goal and go about trying to succeed at that one. We are always striving for success, moving the goalposts whenever we hit a milestone. That is the nature of progress. When a person succeeds at a goal and then stops setting new ones, they clearly are done with that skill or job. If you were learning to play the guitar, and your first goal was to learn how to play one song, you would learn that song fairly quickly. What do you do next? Do you stop playing? Do you put down the guitar forever, comfortable with learning just that one song? If you hated playing, then probably. But if you enjoyed yourself, then you would try to learn another song, and another. In this way, the true definition of success is always changing. If you are always succeeding and then moving on to do more, then how do you bring yourself to feel successful?

This is a struggle that many people experience. The way to deal with it is to form your positive mindset. With this positive mindset, you are able to look toward the future with optimism. You are able to set goals with improvement in mind. You probably wouldn't stop playing your guitar after one song, because even if that one song wasn't very fun, you would go looking for different ones that were fun. With a positive mindset, success becomes a part of life. It's not something to chase, but something you have, simply because you are happy with your place in life. Success means that even when you do fail, you can get back up and start over. Failure is natural, and everyone fails from time to time. It's how you respond to it that's important. Do you keep trying, learning lessons with every failed attempt? Or do you give up, decide the task just isn't for you, and move on to something else? A person with a positive mindset does the former.

A positive mindset can indeed bring you massive success, but it requires constant practice and application. It's an ongoing process that needs to be maintained. It should be in your nature, and not just something that you turn to when things go wrong. In establishing your positive mindset, what you really need to do is develop habits. As you go about the practices in this book, the most important thing to do is to repeat them regularly. It will be hard to meditate at first. It will be hard to identify your negative thoughts, to get used to journaling, to learn your NLP techniques. Changing your entire mindset does not happen in a day, but it will happen. The more you repeat your practices, the more often you do them, and the more regular they become, the better you will get at them. Practice makes perfect. As you practice, your deliberate struggles will become passive habits. You don't need to remind yourself how to brush your teeth. With enough practice, you won't need to remind yourself how to meditate—I don't. My greatest hope is that someday, you don't either.

I wrote this book because I want to show other people how to stay positive, no matter what life throws at them. As difficult as that is, it is possible. And, once you are positive in every situation, you can achieve any goal you can imagine. Your possibilities will be endless. The world will throw hurdles at you, just like before, but instead of tripping and knocking them over, you'll leap over them like they're a small bump in the road. We live in a turbulent, unpredictable world. Disasters, natural and manmade, are commonplace. If you approach this time with your positive mindset, you will be one of the few that are unfazed in all this chaos. That is the greatest skill anyone can have. It doesn't come free; it takes a lot of hard work, dedication, and discipline. But, if you can work your way through all of these steps, you will emerge capable of more than you have ever imagined.

The only thing stopping you from total personal success is you. You have the power to change your life. You have the resources to shift your view of the world. You have everything that you need to transform your mind and take control of your success. It doesn't matter how bad you've faltered in the past. If you make the right choices for your life, then everything else will eventually fall into place. Today, choose to live your life with a positive mindset. It will take you a long time to develop all the skills you need to transform your mindset, but once you choose to embark on this journey, the only thing between you and a permanent change is time. When you make the effort to shift how you think, you are guaranteed to see results. It may take some time, and it will definitely take effort, but it is worth it to see just how bright life is when your mindset is completely positive. Set yourself up for a lifetime of success, happiness, and triumph. Give yourself the gift of a positive mindset, and witness just how much freedom you gain.

# Welcome to the BONUS page! Visit MindsetMultiplied.Com to claim now!

## >>FREE BONUS<<

Thank you again for downloading this book!

I hope this book was able to help you to know how to develop a positive mindset.

The next step is to practice what you have learnt in this book. This is crucial because it does not matter how many books you read but as long as you don't do anything about the information you gain, then you are wasting your time so do something about the information you have received from this book.

Finally, if you enjoyed this book, would you be kind enough to leave a review.

Thank you and good luck!

## References

Deschene, L. (2010, January 11). *7 ways to get past tough situations quickly*. Tiny Buddha. https://tinybuddha.com/blog/7-ways-to-get-past-tough-situations-quickly/

*Inspirational quotes*. (2019). Goodreads.Com. https://www.goodreads.com/quotes/tag/inspirational

Kinderman, P., Schwannauer, M., Pontin, E., & Tai, S. (2013). Psychological processes mediate the impact of familial risk, social circumstances and life events on mental health. *PLoS ONE*, 8(10), e76564. https://doi.org/10.1371/journal.pone.0076564

www.ingramcontent.com/pod-product-compliance
Lightning Source LLC
Chambersburg PA
CBHW071724170526
45165CB00005B/2151